KU-773-104

COST OF LIVING
INDEX NUMBERS

PRACTICE, PRECISION, AND THEORY

STATISTICS

Textbooks and Monographs

A SERIES EDITED BY

D. B. OWEN, Coordinating Editor
Department of Statistics
Southern Methodist University
Dallas, Texas

PAUL D. MINTON
Virginia Commonwealth University
Richmond, Virginia

JOHN W. PRATT
Harvard University
Boston, Massachusetts

OTHER VOLUMES IN PREPARATION

COST OF LIVING
INDEX NUMBERS

PRACTICE, PRECISION, AND THEORY

Kali S. Banerjee

Department of Statistics & Computer Science
University of Delaware
Newark, Delaware

MARCEL DEKKER, INC. New York

EDINBURGH UNIVERSITY LIBRARY
WITHDRAWN

Copyright © 1975 by MARCEL DEKKER, INC.

ALL RIGHTS RESERVED

Neither this book nor any part may be reproduced or transmitted
in any form or by any means, electronic or mechanical, including
photocopying, microfilming, and recording, or by any information
storage and retrieval system, without permission in writing from
the publisher.

MARCEL DEKKER, INC.
270 Madison Avenue, New York, New York 10016

LIBRARY OF CONGRESS CATALOG CARD NUMBER: 75-985

ISBN: 0-8247-6266-5

Current printing (last digit):
10 9 8 7 6 5 4 3 2 1

PRINTED IN THE UNITED STATES OF AMERICA

To my mother, Rajabala
and my father, Heramba Chandra

CONTENTS

Part II

PRECISION AND THEORY

Appendixes

In this monograph, the subject of cost of living index numbers is gradually developed, starting from the definition and providing, in the sequel, the essential features of the subject, mainly in a descriptive manner.

The text is divided into two parts, Part I and Part II. The two chapters of Part I are of a general nature, while the three Chapters of Part II deal with special topics.

Chapter 1 starts from the definition of index numbers and shows how cost of living index numbers are constructed in practice. This Chapter is nonmathematical and illustrates the different stages of computation.

Cost of living index numbers are constructed in government departments, commercial firms, and other institutions all over the world, and in such places a large primary staff is required to work in price collection or in the routine computation of the index. Chapter 1 has been prepared with a view toward introducing the problem of constructing index numbers to such personnel.

Chapter 2 includes a discussion of the formal tests basic in the theory of index numbers, an explanation of the meaning

of the chain index, a description of the components of error
associated with index numbers, and a few other points that are
important for an intelligent appreciation of the formulas.

Chapter 3 explains how index numbers can be constructed
over geographical areas at one point of time, and briefly out-
lines the difficulties associated with the problem.

Chapter 4 provides an introduction to the concept of true
index. An explanation of the basic ideas and the preliminary
concepts of econometrics that are necessary for an understand-
ing of the true index leads up to the derivation of the true
index as formulated by Professor A. Wald. The formula given
by the double-expenditure method of Professor Ragnar Frisch is
also introduced. Finally, this Chapter provides details for
constructing the true index through the factorial approach.

Chapter 5 deals with certain aspects of sampling that may
be required in constructing cost of living index numbers. It
is shown in this chapter how the constituent items of a composite commodity can be sampled for inclusion in the construction of the index and also how sampling errors can be calculated
under such sampling procedures.

Six appendixes comprise the final portion of the book.
Worthy of mention is Appendix A, which is on Divisia's differential derivation of the index. The remaining appendixes deal
with special topics.

Although primarily meant for beginners, this volume may
also be helpful as an introduction to others who may later want
to make a comprehensive study of the subject matter.

As a visiting lecturer at the ISEC (International Statistical Education Centre) of the Indian Statistical Institute,
Calcutta, I taught a service course on cost of living index
numbers. The lectures touched mainly on the practical aspects
of the problem, embodying my own experience as a deputy-
director of the State Statistical Bureau, Calcutta, India.

Later, I was given the privilege of teaching a one-semester
course entirely on index numbers at the New York State School
of Industrial and Labor Relations, Cornell University and
at the Department of Statistics and Computer Science of the
University of Delaware. This text is derived mainly from the
lectures given at Calcutta, Cornell, and Delaware.

In many countries, the expression "cost of living index
(CLI) numbers" is used to mean consumer price index (CPI) numbers,
although gradually the expression CLI is being replaced by CPI.
However, the expression CLI has been retained throughout this
text, except where the expression CPI is used to avoid confusion.

The earliest index number on record appears to be the one
given by Carli of Italy. In order to determine the purchasing
power of money in 1750 compared to that in 1500, Carli (1764)
furnished an index number for prices based on only three commodities, grain, wine, and oil. There has since been an enor-
mous accumulation of literature in this area.

From about the 1920s, the intriguing problem of constructing the true index of cost of living has seriously engaged the
attention of many great men of learning. I have attempted in
the following pages, not a theoretical treatment of what these
eminent scholars said about the complexities of the problem
(which, of course, would be extremely difficult to do), but
some account of the practical or statistical aspects of the
problem with occasional reference to the relevant work of some
of these scholars. However, any views expressed in this monograph are entirely my own.

I am aware of three excellent books on the subject, one by
Mr. B. D. Mudgett, one by Dr. E von Hofsten, and a third by
Dr. M. J. Ulmer, the latter two dealing with special topics.
This volume is in no way a substitute for any of these books,
although an attempt has been made to include in this monograph
the gist of some of the elements featured in those texts.

ACKNOWLEDGMENTS

Grateful thanks are due to Shri A. C. Roy of the Indian Administrative Service, the then Director of the State Statistical Bureau, Government of West Bengal, India, for the encouragement he has given me to prepare a monograph on this subject.

Of numerous well wishers in India and in the U.S.A. to whom I owe a debt of gratitude, I would like to mention particularly Professor R. C. Bose, now at Colorado State University, Professors P. J. McCarthy, I. Blumen, and W. T. Federer of Cornell University, Professor H. C. Fryer of Kansas State University, Professor D. B. Owen of Southern Methodist University, Professors D. E. Lamb and J. F. Leathrum of the University of Delaware, and Dr. J. R. Moore of Aberdeen Proving Ground.

Typing assistance rendered by Mrs. E. Maybee of Cornell at the preparatory stage is also gratefully acknowledged.

COST OF LIVING INDEX NUMBERS

PRACTICE, PRECISION, AND THEORY

Part I

PRACTICE

Chapter 1

INDEX NUMBER FORMULAS AND PRACTICAL DETAILS
FOR CONSTRUCTING COST OF LIVING INDEX NUMBERS

1.1. MEANING AND DEFINITION OF INDEX NUMBERS

An index is something that indicates, and an index number
is an expression of what is to be indicated.

Let p_0 and p_1 be the prices per unit quantity of a
commodity during the time periods "0" and "1," respectively.
The price in the period 1, reduced to a percentage of the price
in the period 0, is given by

$$\frac{100p_1}{p_0} \tag{1.1}$$

If we consider a series of prices p_0, p_1, p_2, ..., p_n in
the periods 0, 1, 2, ..., n, the series of prices in the periods 1, 2, ..., n can be expressed as percentages of the price
in the period 0 as $100p_1/p_0$, $100p_2/p_0$, ..., $100p_n/p_0$ to show
the trend of change in the prices. Each of these percentages
is an index number, because it shows the change of price over
that in the period 0. If we take the index number for the

period 0 as 100, the series of index numbers becomes 100,
$100p_1/p_0$, $100p_2/p_0$, ..., $100p_n/p_0$. This series shows the movement of the price of the commodity under examination. The
period 0 is called the base period, or the period of reference,
and the periods 1, 2, ..., n are the periods of comparison.

1.2. NUMERICAL ILLUSTRATION

Let us suppose that we are interested in the movement of
the price of milk; let us suppose further that the price of
milk in August 1939 was $0.25 and that in May 1954 it was $0.38
per half-gallon. The change in price from August 1939 to May
1954 is $0.38 - $0.25 = $0.13. The price of milk has advanced
from $0.25 to $0.38.

Let us consider simultaneously the price of another commodity, say meat, during these two periods and let the prices
in August 1939 and in May 1954 be $0.87 and $1.00 per pound,
respectively. Notice that, in the case of meat, the increase
in price is also $0.13 per pound. But this increase does not
have the same significance in both cases. The change from $0.25
to $0.38 has a greater significance than the change from $0.87
to $1.00. A comparison of the significance can be made by re-
ducing the price changes to percentages. If we take $0.25 as
equivalent to 100, $0.38 would mean $(0.38/0.25) \times 100 = 152$.
In the same way, $1.00 would be 115 referred to $0.87 as 100.

The index number for the price of milk in May 1954 can be
taken as 152 compared to that in August 1939 taken as 100. Similarly, the price index for meat (i.e., the index number for
the price of meat) in May 1954 is 115 compared to the index in
August 1939 counted as 100. The index numbers of the price for
milk are 100 and 152, and those for meat are 100 and 115, respectively. These numbers show the change of price of the two
commodities over time.

It can be seen from the above that comparability of the
price changes is made possible by reduction to percentage. Percentage makes possible the comparison of the prices per unit,
not only of commodities selling by the same unit of measurement,
but also of commodities selling by different units of measurement, for example, pound for one commodity and kilogram for another, or pair for the third, and so on. Further, it is immaterial whether the price is expressed in dollars, shillings,
crowns, or rupees.

1.3.   DIFFICULTIES INVOLVED IN CONSTRUCTING COST OF LIVING INDEX NUMBERS

In Secs. 1.1 and 1.2, the meaning of index numbers is explained with reference to price. The index numbers for milk
and meat during May 1954 are 152 and 115, respectively. If we
want an idea of the increase in the general price level during
the period on the basis of information furnished by these two
commodities only, the obvious suggestion is to find some sort
of average of 152 and 115, combining the two figures into one.
To add to the complication, let us suppose that there are three
qualities of meat which sell at different prices. There will
therefore be as many series of prices, and consequently as many
series of indexes, for meat as there are qualities. The question then arises as to how to combine these indexes into one
figure to show the change in the general price level.

We have so far been thinking in terms of two commodities
only. It is obvious that only two commodities could not ordinarily claim the representativeness required to show the change
in the general price level. The number of commodities would
have to be increased. Complication would therefore go on in-
creasing with the increase in the number of commodities. If
each such commodity had a different grade or quality, there
would be further complication.

In the present context, we are not interested in measuring the change in the general price level. Instead, we want to measure the change in cost of living of a given class of families. For the purpose of constructing cost of living index[*] numbers, therefore, we do not need to consider prices of all commodities. We need to consider the prices of consumer goods only, that is, goods (and services) that are consumed by a given class of families. The change in the level of retail prices of such consumer goods reflects the change in the cost of living. Retail prices are taken into account because purchases were made by a family at retail rates.

The cost on account of milk and meat no doubt contributes to living cost, but there are numerous other commodities, the consumption of which contributes to the cost of living. A question then arises as to how many and what types of commodities should be included in the construction and, if it is not possible to include all such commodities, how the selection should be made.

Further, the contribution of an item of consumption to living cost depends, no only on the price of the commodity, but also on the quantity consumed. For instance, milk may be consumed in larger quantities than meat. The expenditure on milk may therefore be more than that on meat. Milk may thus have a greater importance or weight in the consumption.

The issues raised above are only some of those that afford an idea of the difficulties associated with the construction of cost of living index numbers.

---

[*] The expression "cost of living index" is being gradually replaced by expressions like "consumer price index" or "retail price index." But in this text the expression cost of living index is used throughout to mean consumer price index.

1.4. DERIVATION OF FORMULAS FOR COMPUTING COST OF LIVING
      INDEX NUMBERS FROM A PRIORI CONSIDERATIONS

Whenever there is a reference to the cost of living index,
it must be understood that it is associated with a well-defined
class of people, the class of people to which the cost of living
would relate: the middle class, the working class, or any other
class of a community. A class defined as middle class may be
too broad; in that case, the class may have to be stratified by
"expenditure levels."

Let us suppose that it is possible to determine the quantities of all items consumed by an average family of a well-
defined class of people. Let, also, the prices of the items be
known. If q_0 represents the quantity of an item consumed in
the period 0, and p_0 denotes the corresponding price, the
total cost in the period 0 is given by

$$\Sigma \, p_0 q_0 \qquad\qquad\qquad (1.2)$$

where the summation Σ extends over all the items consumed.
Expression (1.2) is, in fact, an abbreviation for

$$\sum_{i=1}^{N} p_{0i} q_{0i} \qquad\qquad\qquad (1.3)$$

where Σ extends to all the N items consumed in the period 0,
and p_{0i} and q_{0i} represent, respectively, the price and the
quantity of the ith item.

It is therefore clear that, given the prices and the quantities consumed in a given period, it is possible to evaluate
the total cost of living in that period. Thus, $\Sigma \, p_0 q_0$ represents the cost of living in the period 0. If the same quantities q_0 are priced with the prices p_1, that is, the prices
that ruled in the period 1, the total cost of living in the
period 1 is given by $\Sigma \, p_1 q_0$. Compared to the cost in the period 0, the cost in the period 1 can be expressed in percentage
as

$$\frac{100 \, \Sigma \, p_1 q_0}{\Sigma \, p_0 q_0} \tag{1.4}$$

Expression (1.4) is the cost of living index number for the
period 1 compared to the period 0.

The above index is, in fact, a comparison of two costs.
The comparison has taken the form of expressing one cost as a
percentage of the other. The quantities q_0 (i.e., the quantities consumed in the period 0) have been priced in the two
periods. For the same purpose, one could also use the quantities q_1 (i.e., the quantities consumed in the period 1) rather
than q_0. Situations might arise when, indeed, the quantities
q_1 would be preferred. Without going into further questions
at this stage, we can state that one might adopt q_1 just as
well. If q_1 were taken as the quantities to be priced with
the prices prevailing in the periods 0 and 1, the cost of living index number for the period 1 compared to the period 0 would
take the form

$$\frac{100 \, \Sigma \, p_1 q_1}{\Sigma \, p_0 q_1} \tag{1.5}$$

Indexes (1.4) and (1.5) emerge from two distinct considerations. In (1.4), q_0 is evaluated while, in (1.5), q_1 is
evaluated. These two formulas separately afford the required
comparison of the price level, but they might give rise to two
different index numbers for the same comparison. A question
then arises as to which of the two should be accepted as correct.
An average of the two indexes can immediately be suggested as
a compromise. A geometric average of the two is given by

$$100 \left(\frac{\Sigma \, p_1 q_0}{\Sigma \, p_0 q_0} \frac{\Sigma \, p_1 q_1}{\Sigma \, p_0 q_1} \right)^{1/2} \tag{1.6}$$

Formula (1.4) is known as Laspeyres' formula,[*] (1.5) is
Paasche's formula,[†] and (1.6) is the ideal formula of Irving
Fisher[‡] [30].

There are, in fact, other forms of compromise and many
other formulas [30]   Some of these forms are the following:

$$\frac{100}{2} \left(\frac{\Sigma\, p_1 q_0}{\Sigma\, p_0 q_0} + \frac{\Sigma\, p_1 q_1}{\Sigma\, p_0 q_1} \right) \tag{1.7}$$

$$\frac{100\, \Sigma\, p_1(q_0 + q_1)}{\Sigma\, p_0(q_0 + q_1)} \tag{1.8}$$

$$\frac{100\, \Sigma\, (q_0 q_1)^{1/2}\, p_1}{\Sigma\, (q_0 q_1)^{1/2}\, p_0} \tag{1.9}$$

Forms (1.7) through (1.9) suggest that each is some sort of
average of the indexes of Laspeyres and Paasche. Formula (1.8)
is known as the Marshall-Edgeworth formula.

The compromises so far indicated are based on the quantities q_0 and q_1, i.e., the quantities consumed in the periods
0 and 1. Instead of thinking in terms of a compromise between
the quantities q_0 and q_1, we could just as well suggest a
formula such as

$$\frac{100\, \Sigma\, p_1 q_a}{\Sigma\, p_0 q_a} \tag{1.10}$$

---

[*] E. Laspeyres used this formula in 1864.

[†] The formula was used by H. Paasche in 1874.

[‡] This formula was "considered by Bowley, recommended by
Walsh and Pigou, and called by Fisher the ideal formula" (R.
Frish, p. 6, ref. [32]).

where the quantities q_a are kept fixed and are obtained as the averages of quantities consumed over a number of years. If Laspeyres' formula were used for a number of years without any change in the quantities q_0 , it would be equivalent to using a formula with fixed quantities as in the form (1.10), although the quantities q_0 would not actually be the averages drawn over a number of years.

The above formulas are deduced from general considerations. Some of them can also be deduced from other considerations (Appendix A).

A question may arise as to which of these formulas should be accepted as the best. The superiority of one formula over another is judged on the basis of certain tests which are basic in the theory of index numbers and which are discussed in Chapter 2. (Irving Fisher has discussed the merits of an amazing number of index number formulas in his text, The Making of Index Numbers [30]. All students of index numbers should examine this book carefully.)

1.5. SIMPLIFICATION OF THE FORMULA TO WORKABLE FORM

The actual computation of cost of living index numbers will be illustrated with reference to formula (1.4), Laspeyres' formula, since in most countries[*] it is used to provide cost of living index numbers.

Construction of cost of living index numbers by this formula, as by any other, necessitates obtaining information on the quantities (quantities consumed per average family) of the items. But it is difficult in practice to find such average quantities of consumption in all cases. To meet this difficulty,

---

[*]See p. 74 of ref. [37].

the formulas can be reduced to forms in which information on
the quantities consumed is not directly involved.

Expression (1.4) can be written in the form

$$\frac{100 \sum p_{1i} q_{0i}}{\sum p_{0i} q_{0i}} \qquad (1.11)$$

where the subscripts i have the same meaning as in expression
(1.3). Expression (1.11) can be reduced to the form

$$\frac{100 \sum (p_{1i}/p_{0i})\, p_{0i} q_{0i}}{\sum p_{0i} q_{0i}} \qquad (1.12)$$

In expression (1.12), the denominator $\sum p_{0i} q_{0i}$ is fixed, because it represents the total cost in the period 0. Therefore,
$(p_{0i} q_{0i})/\sum p_{0i} q_{0i}$ represents the proportion of cost that the
ith item would bear on the total cost in the period 0. If we
denote $100 p_{1i}/p_{0i}$ by r_i , and $p_{0i} q_{0i}/\sum p_{0i} q_{0i}$ by w_i , expression (1.12) can be reduced to

$$\sum r_i w_i \qquad (1.13)$$

where r_i is the _price_ _relative_ of the ith item, and w_i is
its _weight_.

Expression (1.13) is easily recognized as a weighted average of price relatives. It is immaterial whether $\sum w_i$ is
placed in the denominator, since $\sum w_i = 1$.

In practice, weights are expressed in percentages and not
in proportions of unity. In that case, the index number is

$$\sum \frac{r_i w_i}{100}$$

or, more appropriately,

$$\frac{\sum r_i w_i}{\sum w_i} \qquad (1.14)$$

Either of the above forms, namely (1.13) or (1.14), clearly shows that the cost of living index number is, by reduction, a weighted average of price relatives. Therefore, direct use of the quantities is not involved in any of the above forms.

1.6. QUANTITY INDEX

Any of the formulas in Sec. 1.4, which may be adopted for the construction of price index, may also be suitably adapted to the construction of <u>quantity index</u>. These formulas give a measurement of the movement of prices. With a little orientation, they can be made to measure the movement (or change) in quantities.

The numerator and the denominator of any of these formulas are aggregates, each giving the total cost of the commodities consumed. Both prices and quantities appear jointly in the aggregate and play, as it were, a complementary role. It therefore appears that the formula designed to measure change in prices might also be adapted to measure change in quantities. In fact, it is possible to do so by allowing quantity to take the place of price, and price that of quantity. Let us take formula (1.4) as an illustration. An equivalent formula for quantity index can be derived from (1.4) by changing p to q, and q to p. The formula then reduces to

$$\frac{100 \sum q_1 p_0}{\sum q_0 p_0} = \frac{100 \sum (q_1/q_0) \, p_0 q_0}{\sum p_0 q_0} \tag{1.15}$$

Reduced to a workable form similar to that for the price index as shown in Sec. 1.5, the above formula would take the form of a weighted average of quantity relatives. The weight associated with a quantity relative of an item is given by the percentage value of the item concerned. The construction of

quantity index is useful, for instance, in the field of industrial production. The quantity relative is the relative of
production, and the weight is given by its percentage value.
This value may be taken, for example, as the value added by
manufacture, or some other appropriate weighting system may be
adopted. (We will not, however, enter into any detailed discussion of quantity index in this text.)

1.7.   DIVISION OF TOTAL CONSUMPTION INTO MAJOR GROUPS

It has been almost conventional in some places to compute
the cost of living index number under five major groups of consumption. According to necessity, any of the major groups can
be divided into subgroups. We shall, however, confine our discussion to the following five major groups of consumption:
(a) food,   (b) fuel and light,   (c) clothing,   (d) housing, and
(e) miscellaneous.

It might be necessary to compute the cost of living index
separately for each individual group or for a combination of
some, or all, of these five major groups. We shall, in the
first instance, indicate the computation of the index for food.

It has been seen that, if an item of consumption is to be
included in the construction, it is necessary to know both its
price relative and the weight. The prices of all items, big
and small, of food consumed have to be obtained for both the
base period and the period compared, and the price relatives
must be calculated from the prices in the two periods. But each
of these price relatives cannot be used individually in the
construction, unless the corresponding weight is also known.
However insignificant an item of consumption is, it may not be
difficult to ascertain its price and hence to calculate the
price relative, but it may be difficult to find its weight.

It has been stated before that the weight of an item is the proportion of its expenditure to total expenditure. Information on such expenditure is collected from a family budget enquiry,[*] (consumer expenditure survey), reference to which is made in Sec. 1.14. Weights that are made available by a consumer expenditure survey (family budget inquiry) are usually related to composite commodities. When the corresponding price relatives are available, the computation of the index is simple, as shown in the next section.

1.8. COMPUTATION OF THE INDEX

The actual computation of the cost of living index with respect to food is illustrated here with reference to a given expenditure level of a given class of families. The individual weights and the price relatives are shown in Table 1.1. The weights are being used for illustrative purposes only. (In fact, the weighting pattern would change with the pattern of consumption of the class of families for which the cost of living index is required.)

The products of the weights and the price relatives are shown in the fourth column. The sum of these products divided by the sum of the weights, which in this case is 100, gives the index on food as 91.4.

The indexes for the other major groups can be similarly calculated, and the group indexes can be combined into the overall index, as shown in Table 1.2. Notice that the sum of the group weights (shown in the second column) is 100. The group

---

[*] The expression "family budget enquiry" has been in use in international literature but, in some places, the word "inquiry," rather than "enquiry," is preferred.

indexes are entered in the third column. Here, a group index
is, in fact, a price relative for the group. The product of
the group weights and the group indexes is shown in the fourth
column. The sum of the products divided by the total weight
gives the index number combined for all the groups. This combined index is the required cost of living index.

The index for the cost on food, which is a major group, is
calculated in a similar manner as shown in Table 1.1. There
also, the sum of weights for the individual items (i.e., items
under food) is 100. Similarly, the total weight in any other
major group can be taken as 100. In other words, the expenditure in a major group distributes itself in percentages among
the constituent items of the group. The group weights are,
again, a percentage distribution of the total expenditure among
the groups. Therefore, the group weights also add up to 100
(see subsection 1.12).

The index according to formula (1.14) is a weighted average
of the price relatives. A direct one-stage calculation is implied in the formula, but here the index is calculated in two
stages. The first stage gives a group index, and the second
gives the overall index. Direct calculation and calculation by
stages lead to identical results, as is evident from the algebraic simplification given below.

The formula for the index number is given by

$$\frac{\sum r_i w_i}{\sum w_i} \tag{1.16}$$

where $\sum w_i$ is the sum of five group weights, $\sum_1 w_i$, $\sum_2 w_i$, $\cdots$,
$\sum_5 w_i$, corresponding to the five groups. That is, we can write

$$\sum w_i = \sum_1 w_i + \sum_2 w_i + \cdots + \sum_5 w_i,$$

where each of $\sum_1$, $\sum_2$, $\ldots$, $\sum_5$ is, in turn, the sum of weights
of the individual items of the group concerned.

TABLE 1.1

Cost of Living Index of Food Under a Given Expenditure Level
of a Given Class of Families in an Asiatic City During
December 1953[a]

Items	Price relative	Weight	Weight × price relative
1. Cereals (of a particular kind)	102	27.64	2819
2. Processed cereals (of a special kind)	86	1.99	171
3. Wheat and wheat products other than those above (1 and 2)	125	8.28	1035
4. Other cereals and cereal products	95	0.72	68
5. Pulses	91	5.09	463
6. Edible oils	72	7.93	571
7. Vegetable oil (of a special kind other than in item 6)	102	0.93	95
8. Salt	92	0.41	38
9. Spices	85	3.93	334
10. Sugar	93	4.67	434
11. Nonrefined sugar	123	0.56	69
12. Milk	101	3.44	347
13. Butter and whipped butter	95	0.71	67
14. Other milk products	96	0.63	60
15. Potatoes	62	4.13	256
16. Onions	155	0.69	107
17. Other nonleafy vegetables	57	8.31	474
18. Leafy vegetables	83	3.47	288
19. Fish	76	7.54	573

TABLE 1.1 CONTINUED

	Items	Price relative	Weight	Weight × price relative
20.	Meat	97	1.74	169
21.	Eggs	80	0.39	31
22.	Fruit	107	1.17	125
23.	Tea and coffee	101	1.34	135
24.	Refreshments (other than those mentioned above)	90	3.20	288
25.	Other food materials	116	1.09	126
	Index for food		100.00	9143
				91.4

[a]Taken from published reports of the government of West Bengal, India [58]. The names of some of the items of consumption have been written differently. (Base: November 1950 = 100.)

TABLE 1.2

Cost of Living Index of a Given Class of Families at a
Given Expenditure Level in December 1953[a]

Major groups of consumption	For the given expenditure level		
	Weight	Index during December 1953	Weight × index
Food	58.55	91.4	5351.5
Clothing	5.37	106.5	571.9
Fuel and light	6.15	102.2	628.5
Housing	9.61	100.0	961.0
Miscellaneous	20.32	100.3	2038.1
All combined	100.00		95.5

[a] Taken from published reports of the Government of West Bengal, India [58]. (Base: November 1950 = 100.)

The overall index from the five group indexes is given by

$$\frac{R_1 \sum_1 w_i + R_2 \sum_2 w_i + \cdots + R_5 \sum_5 w_i}{\sum_1 w_i + \sum_2 w_i + \cdots + \sum_5 w_i} \qquad (1.17)$$

where R_1, R_2, ..., R_5 are the following group indexes:

$$R_1 = \frac{\sum_1 r_i w_i}{\sum_1 w_i}, \quad R_2 = \frac{\sum_2 r_i w_i}{\sum_2 w_i}, \quad \ldots, \quad R_5 = \frac{\sum_5 r_i w_i}{\sum_5 w_i}$$

The numerator in a group index is the sum of the products of the price relatives and the weights of the individual items of that group. Hence, $\sum r_i w_i = \sum_1 r_i w_i + \sum_2 r_i w_i + \cdots + \sum_5 r_i w_i$

If we substitute the values of R_1, R_2, ..., R_5 in the numerator of (1.17), the numerator reduces to

$$\sum_1 r_i w_i + \sum_2 r_i w_i + \cdots + \sum_5 r_i w_i$$

Thus, expression (1.17) is equal to

$$\frac{\sum_1 r_i w_i + \sum_2 r_i w_i + \cdots + \sum_5 r_i w_i}{\sum w_i}$$

$$= \frac{\sum r_i w_i}{\sum w_i}$$

which is the same as expression (1.16).

Tables 1.3 and 1.4 provide an idea of how weights might differ from place to place.

TABLE 1.3
Weights for the United States[a]

Group	Number of Items	Percentage Weight
Food	105	22.5
Housing:		
Shelter (rent, home ownership, and maintenance and repairs)	18	20.2
Fuels and utilities	10	5.2
Household furnishings and operation	53	7.7
Clothing	77	10.6
Transportation	34	13.9
Medical care	38	5.8
Personal care	12	2.8
Reading and recreation	34	6.0
Other	15	5.3
Total	396	100.0

[a]Source: ref. 38. (Official base: 1967 = 100.)

TABLE 1.4

Weights for the United Kingdom[a]

Group	Number of Items	Percentage Weight (1972)[b]
Food	150	25.1
Meals taken outside home		4.6
Alcoholic drinks	4	6.6
Tobacco	2	5.3

Housing
  Rent (including owner-occupied
    dwellings)
  Repairs and maintenance
  Rates and water charges
	1
	5
	1
		7.1
		1.9
		3.1

Fuel and light	5	6.0
Clothing	64	8.9
Durable household goods	49	5.8
Transport and vehicles	16	13.9
Miscellaneous goods	31	6.5
Services	20	5.2
Total	348	100.0

[a]Source: Ref. [38]. (Offical base: January 1962 = 100.)

[b]The weights are revised each January on the basis of a continuing family expenditure survey.

1.9. TREATMENT OF COMPOSITE COMMODITIES

In a schedule of items on food, vegetables appear as an
item. "Vegetables" is a composite commodity and has numerous
constituent items. It can be subdivided into leafy vegetables
and nonleafy vegetables, and nonleafy vegetables can be divided
into, say, potatoes and the rest of the nonleafy items, or into
any other subdivisions, depending on the nature and importance
of the items to be grouped together. Such items as leafy vegetables, potatoes, etc., are also composite in character, because
there may be several varieties of leafy vegetables, several
varieties of potatoes, and so on. The constituent items of a
commodity such as leafy vegetables may be so numerous that it
will be hardly feasible to find out separately the expenditures,
and therefore, the weights, on all the constituent items of
this commodity. But it may not be difficult to collect information on the expenditure on all leafy vegetables put together
from a family budget inquiry.

It can thus be seen that, although the prices, and therefore the price relatives, might be available for all the constituent items of a composite commodity, it may not be possible
to utilize individually all the price relatives for want of the
corresponding weights.

When the weight is available for a composite commodity
like vegetables or leafy vegetables, either of two methods may
be adopted in practice for calculating the price relative for
the composite commodity.

One method is to work with the average of the price relatives of the constituent items. Another is to work with the
price relative of the average prices of the composite commodity.
In both cases, one price relative is obtained to correspond to
one weight.

In circumstances where it is not possible to get a dependable average price for the composite commodity, the former

procedure, namely that of working with an average of the price
relatives, can be adopted. A simple arithmetic mean of the
price relatives can be taken [7]. (For the theoretical justification of this method, see Chapter 5 and Appendix D.)

The prices of the constituent items of a composite commodity may vary considerably from one item to another. Quantities sold may also differ widely from item to item. If, however, it were possible to collect information on the quantities
of the items sold while collecting the price quotations, it
would be possible to find a weighted average price of the composite commodity, that is, an average price weighted with the
quantities sold. An average price of a composite commodity
obtained as such is a dependable average [8, 53] price for the
composite commodity. (For the rationale of this procedure, see
Appendix B.)

1.10.   CALCULATION OF AVERAGE PRICES AND
THE PRICE RELATIVES

Table 1.5 is a summary of the quantities sold and the
price quotations of the subitems under a composite commodity.
It can be seen that there are 51 items constituting this composite commodity. The fourth column shows sales (representative sales in representative markets) for each item. The value
aggregate is given in the fifth column. The totals of these
two columns are indicated at the bottom of the table. The
weighted average price per weight unit calculated from these
totals is 0.29 of the currency. The corresponding weighted
average price during the base period is 0.35 of the currency.
The price relative is therefore 83 as shown in footnote a.

It can be seen that the base period prices of some of the
items were not available. Since the prices of only 36 items

TABLE 1.5

Weighted Average Prices of the Items of a Composite Commodity During December 1953 and their Relatives with the Corresponding Prices in the Base Period[a]

Sl. no. of the Items	Total no. of markets where available	No. of quotations	Total quantities sold (weight units)	Value (in currency)	Weighted average price in Dec. 1953 (per weight unit)	Weighted average price in the base period, Nov. 1953 (per weight unit)	Price relative
1	1	1	2.00	0.50	0.25	-	-
2	11	53	135.00	96.62	0.68	0.12	567
3	5	40	600.00	190.79	0.32	0.06	533
4	21	120	1104.62	253.38	0.23	0.22	105
5	1	6	3.75	3.01	0.80	1.25	64
6	23	91	817.50	134.18	0.16	0.24	67
7	2	7	42.00	10.75	0.26	-	-
8	21	315	1527.00	529.64	0.35	0.66	53
9	4	15	12.75	7.12	0.56	1.00	56
10	5	9	33.00	18.61	0.56	-	-
11	1	1	0.50	0.25	0.50	-	-
12	5	9	39.50	15.64	0.40	1.00	40

TABLE 1.5   CONTINUED

Sl. no. of the Items	Total no. of markets where avail-able	No. of quota-tions	Total quan-tities sold (weight units)	Value (in currency)	Weighted average price in Dec. 1953 (per weight unit)	Weighted average price in the base period, Nov. 1953 (per weight unit)	Price relative
13	14	53	259.00	69.52	0.27	0.23	117
14	15	47	186.00	31.38	0.22	0.27	81
15	3	5	7.00	2.07	0.30	0.38	79
16	6	8	32.00	14.73	0.46	-	-
17	21	90	78.24	49.59	0.63	0.89	71
18	24	1020	2053.42	1157.15	0.56	2.02	28
19	8	18	88.00	22.41	0.25	0.24	104
20	17	35	60.75	37.70	0.62	1.10	56
21	1	19	0.50	0.19	0.38	-	-
22	24	221	210.41	181.70	0.86	1.18	73
23	4	6	30.75	7.84	0.25	0.31	81
24	24	1227	12749.00	1717.42	0.13	0.27	48
25	24	124	1030.00	177.07	0.17	0.20	85
26	22	138	118.47	624.71	5.27	1.45	363

27	4	8	20.75	8.50	0.41	-	-
28	1	2	5.25	1.00	0.19	0.31	61
29	24	574	2234.10	813.68	0.36	0.42	86
30	6	6	56.25	26.94	0.48	-	-
31	13	32	22.25	14.75	0.66	0.45	147
32	24	689	13053.50	4459.53	0.34	0.97	35
33	23	210	790.50	285.62	0.36	-	-
34	23	123	465.00	168.86	0.36	0.67	54
35	17	38	208.00	30.06	0.14	0.26	54
36	24	209	340.74	192.82	0.57	0.91	63
37	11	27	18.11	15.35	0.85	-	-
38	1	1	0.50	0.25	0.50	0.35	143
39	23	212	1906.25	353.73	0.19	0.26	73
40	19	97	511.00	117.46	0.23	0.27	85
41	4	11	94.00	39.81	0.42	-	-
42	4	10	24.25	10.58	0.44	-	-
43	2	3	15.00	5.49	0.37	-	-
44	9	20	57.50	23.09	0.40	0.84	48
45	11	20	342.00	56.40	0.16	-	-
46	2	2	3.00	1.25	0.42	0.22	191

TABLE 1.5 CONTINUED

Sl. no. of the Items	Total no. of markets where available	No. of quotations	Total quantities sold (weight units)	Value (in currency)	Weighted average price in Dec. 1953 (per weight unit)	Weighted average price in the base period, Nov. 1953 (per weight unit)	Price relative
47	24	468	665.47	331.45	0.50	1.29	388
48	19	81	450.00	177.10	0.39	0.30	130
49	9	20	49.81	13.80	0.28	0.25	112
50	22	107	302.25	65.35	0.22	0.40	55
51	4	12	81.00	19.77	0.24	-	-
Total			42938.14	12582.61			

[a](1) Total quantity = 42938.14; (2) total value = 12582.61; (3) weighted average price drawn from 51 items during December 1953 = 0.29; (4) weighted average price during November 1953 (when only 36 items were available) = 0.35; (5) hence, price relative = 83. (6) Arithmetic average of price relatives drawn from the 36 items having prices in the base period = 122; (7) weighted average of the prices of the common 36 items during December 1953 = 0.29; (8) hence, price relative = 83.

were provided, only 36 price relatives could be obtained. An
arithmetic average of these 36 price relatives is 122. This is
much higher than 83.

When the price relative is calculated as the ratio of the
two weighted average prices from the 36 items that are common
in both the periods, it comes out exactly as 83, as shown in
statement (8), footnote a, agreeing with what is shown in statement (5). Fifty-one items in the period of comparison and 36
items in the base period lead, therefore, to the same result
as that obtained with 36 items in both the periods. Although
such a close agreement is quite accidental, it raises the issue
whether even fewer than 36 items would have served the purpose
equally well.

The price relative, 83, can be used in the construction of
the index in view of the nature of the composite commodity (see
Chapter 5 and Appendix B).

1.11 SPECIFICATION OF ITEMS

The specification of an item to be priced is essential.
An item has to be priced according to specification, and the
price relative must be calculated on items of identical specification. If, for instance, the price obtained in the base
period refers to a particular variety of meat, it will be necessary to obtain the price of the same variety of meat in the
periods of comparison. But, in practice, it may be observed
that the particular item (or the quality, or the variety) that
had been priced in the base period disappeared from the market
in a subsequent period.

The disappearance of an item of a given specification is
of frequent occurrence among goods in the miscellaneous group.
Under footwear, prices of shoes can be collected. Usually,

these prices are collected for a standard design, quality, and
size (covered by a commerical number), but the design of shoes
may change considerably and within a short period.

When an item of a given specification priced in the base
period disappears from the market, or when the quality of a
commodity priced in the base period changes, difficulties arise
in calculating the price relative. E. von Hofsten [63] has
discussed this problem at some length. The following is an
interesting example cited by him.

Let us suppose that a variety a which was for sale in
the period 0 has been substituted by the variety b in the
period 1 and that the quality of b is different from that of
a. If p_0^a is the price of a in the period 0 and p_1^b is the
price of b in the period 1, one might be tempted to calculate
the price relative (omitting 100) as

$$\frac{p_1^b}{p_0^a}$$

without any regard for the change in quality that might have
taken place in the meantime. This would obviously be wrong.
If, however, it were possible to estimate the qualities of a
and b on an objective basis and to calculate the ratio of the
qualities, it would be reasonable to adjust the above price relative in accordance with this quality ratio. If g were the
ratio of the quality of b to that of a, it would be appropriate to adjust the price relative as

$$\frac{1}{g} \frac{p_1^b}{p_0^a} \tag{1.18}$$

As an example of such a transition from one variety to
another, von Hofsten cites the situation that arose when the
fat content of milk was reduced in Sweden in the autumn of 1941.

Previously, milk sold for consumption had an average fat content of approximately 3.6% and the price was 30 öre/liter (in
Stockholm). From then on the fat content was standardized at
3.0% and the price was altered to 29 öre/liter. To disregard
the quality change would be equivalent to using the quotient
p_1^b/p_0^a as a measure of price change. In this example, this
method would give 29/30 = 0.97, i.e., a 3% decrease in price.
Obviously, such a procedure would not be desirable.

Let us assume that it is possible in some situations to
compare quantitatively the quality of one article with that of
the other. If the quality of article b is to the quality of
article a as the constant g is to 1, one obtains

$$I_{01} = \frac{1}{g}\ \frac{p_1^b}{p_0^a}$$

as the adjusted price relative.   Von Hofsten reported that this
procedure was used for the official Swedish index in the above-
mentioned situation for milk. The caloric content was taken as
a measure of the milk quality, and it was calculated that the
higher fat content corresponded to 650 and the lower to 600
cal/liter. Consequently, g = 600/650 = 0.923 and, for the
price relative of milk, (1/0.923)(29/30) = 1.05 was used, which
in fact reflected a 5% increase in price.

The above procedure can be recommended only when it is
possible to evaluate the qualities of goods on an objective
basis.   In practice, a method known as the splicing method is
usually adopted to meet such situations. As a rule, a variety
does not disappear suddenly. Before it disappears from the
market completely, it remains available in the market for some
time along with a similar variety by which it is eventually
replaced.

Let us assume that, of the prices p_0^a, p_1^a, p_2^a for the variety a in the periods 0, 1, and 2, the price p_2^a is unknown, because the variety has mean while disappeared. Our aim is to estimate p_2^a/p_0^a. Let us now suppose that the prices of a similar variety b, a close associate of a, are available for the periods 1 and 2, and let these prices be p_1^b and p_2^b. Both a and b appear simultaneously in the period 1. Let us then make either of the following assumptions:

1. The price of a changes from the period 1 to period 2 in the same ratio as the price of b. Symbolically, this assumption means

$$\frac{p_2^a}{p_1^a} = \frac{p_2^b}{p_1^b}$$

2. Or let us assume that the ratio of the prices of a and b in the period 1 is the same as the ratio of the prices of a and b in the period 2. Symbolically, this assumption means

$$\frac{p_1^a}{p_1^b} = \frac{p_2^a}{p_2^b}$$

Since a and b are close associates, either of the assumptions, which are algebraically the same, holds good in general.

From either of these assumptions, we can find out the required price relative in the form

$$\frac{p_2^a}{p_0^a} = \frac{p_1^a}{p_0^a} \frac{p_2^b}{p_1^b} \tag{1.19}$$

The product on the right hand side of the above relationship involves a linking of the price relative of a between
the periods 1 and 0 with the price relative of b between the
periods 2 and 1.

If the quality factor g could be taken as equivalent to
the ratio of the prices of a and b in the period 1, that is,
if it could be assumed that

$$g = \frac{p_1^b}{p_1^a} \qquad\qquad (1.20)$$

formula (1.19) would give the same result as (1.18). In a free
market, prices would perhaps always lead to the equivalence
(1.20). Although there might be objections to the splicing
method, as has been pointed out by E. von Hofsten, this method
can be recommended for all practical purposes wherever feasible.

If one or more varieties or qualities of a composite commodity disappear from the market, there may still remain other
varieties or qualities of the same commodity. In such a situation, it might be preferable to work with the prices of the
existing varieties or qualities of the composite commodity,
ignoring the varieties or the qualities that have gone out of
the market. That is, the price relative may be calculated from
the varieties or qualities still remaining in the market.

1.12. COVERAGE UNDER THE MAJOR GROUPS OF CONSUMPTION

Weights depend on the pattern of consumption, which differs
from people to people and from place to place. Some idea of the
weighting structures relevant to an Asiatic city is provided in
Table 1.4. Table 1.1 illustrates how the food group is covered.
Table 1.6 indicates how other major groups can be covered.

TABLE 1.6

Weights of Different Items of Consumption[a]

Items of consumption	Monthly expenditure levels				
	Level I	Level II	Level III	Level IV	Level V
Food					
Rice (cereals)	27.64	21.90	17.12	13.82	9.19
Processed cereals of special kinds	1.99	2.03	1.87	1.57	1.12
Wheat and wheat products	8.28	7.96	7.12	5.50	4.55
Other cereals and cereal products	0.72	0.52	0.54	0.62	1.03
Pulses	5.09	4.30	4.18	3.47	3.33
Edible oil	7.93	6.60	6.14	5.86	4.85
Vegetable oil	0.93	1.97	2.69	3.38	2.77
Salt	0.41	0.39	0.29	0.30	0.17
Spices	3.93	3.50	3.38	2.99	2.52
Sugar	4.67	4.26	3.81	3.48	2.58
Nonrefined sugar	0.56	0.85	0.80	0.88	1.04
Milk	3.44	7.76	12.02	12.777	14.14
Butter and whipped butter	0.71	2.38	4.20	4.84	8.45
Other milk products	0.63	0.80	1.01	1.43	1.96
Potatoes	4.13	4.46	4.07	3.75	3.61

Onions	0.69	0.50	0.37	0.38	0.39
Other nonleafy vegetables	8.31	8.58	8.40	8.35	7.26
Leafy vegetables	3.47	2.96	2.56	2.59	2.09
Fish	7.54	8.71	8.86	11.00	9.80
Meat	1.74	2.26	2.44	3.63	4.77
Eggs	0.39	0.67	0.70	1.25	1.73
Fruit	1.17	1.91	2.26	2.64	4.12
Tea and coffee	1.34	1.59	1.85	2.15	2.16
Other refreshments	3.20	2.42	2.46	2.73	5.40
Other food materials	1.09	0.72	0.86	0.62	0.97
Total food	100.00	100.00	100.00	100.00	100.00
Fuel and light					
Coal and coke	49.92	41.18	36.96	32.22	31.63
Firewood	10.88	8.44	8.85	10.92	7.50
Other fuels	11.04	15.46	11.77	10.33	6.75
Matches	6.03	4.31	3.90	2.99	2.20
Kerosene	15.77	11.11	6.83	4.58	1.69
Electricity	4.75	18.40	31.31	38.03	50.10
Candles	1.61	1.10	0.38	0.93	0.13
Total fuel and light	100.00	100.00	100.00	100.00	100.00

TABLE 1.6 CONTINUED

Items of consumption	Monthly expenditure levels				
	Level I	Level II	Level III	Level IV	Level V
Clothing					
Men's clothes	44.19	40.30	32.15	34.67	34.95
Women's clothes	39.06	35.31	35.25	37.50	37.48
Children's clothes	9.27	14.78	16.39	15.34	13.84
Unclassified	7.48	9.61	16.21	12.49	13.73
Total clothing	100.00	100.00	100.00	100.00	100.00
Housing					
House rent	89.30	91.79	87.12	81.77	51.80
Taxes	7.24	6.16	9.95	10.11	19.80
House repairing	3.46	2.05	2.93	8.12	28.40
Total housing	100.00	100.00	100.00	100.00	100.00
Miscellaneous					
Chewing materials (after food)	6.02	4.38	3.14	1.90	1.14
Tobacco and cigarettes	10.79	6.95	4.62	3.92	3.44
Washing soda	1.54	0.93	0.44	0.30	0.10

Washing soap	4.83	3.63	2.68	1.70	1.04
Footwear, umbrellas	4.42	4.42	3.47	2.80	2.02
Bedding	0.98	1.17	1.19	1.09	1.02
Furniture	0.20	0.07	0.36	0.80	3.50
Utensils	0.99	0.70	0.62	0.53	0.45
Toilet soap	1.97	1.93	1.60	1.21	0.80
Cream, powder, etc.	0.42	0.72	0.86	0.88	0.80
Hair oil	4.18	3.24	2.35	1.67	0.98
Shaving material	0.46	0.52	0.36	0.34	0.18
Other toilet goods	0.04	0.13	0.13	0.11	0.19
Barber	3.70	2.53	1.70	1.16	0.56
Laundry	2.88	4.05	4.48	3.97	2.63
School and college fees	1.17	4.66	5.53	5.87	2.92
Examination fees	0.16	0.41	0.58	0.61	0.29
Music lessons	0.04	0.15	0.29	0.39	0.41
Newspapers	0.35	1.07	1.76	1.67	0.75
Books	0.45	1.70	2.05	2.09	1.37
Conveyances	10.03	8.91	8.69	8.90	5.83
Medical expenses	6.34	8.05	7.57	9.36	7.73

TABLE 1.6 CONTINUED

Items of consuption	Monthly expenditure levels				
	Level I	Level II	Level III	Level IV	Level V
Miscellaneous continued					
Amusement	3.32	3.72	3.36	3.28	2.86
Travelling expenses	1.99	2.07	2.45	2.52	2.82
Insurance and P. fund	1.47	5.63	9.47	9.35	13.02
Total miscellaneous	68.74	71.74	69.75	66.42	56.85

[a]Taken from published reports of the government of West Bengal, India [58]. The names of some of the items of consumption have been written differently. (Base: November 1950 = 100; center: same as that in Table 1.1.)

(It should be mentioned again that these details are merely illustrative.)

Notice that, in all expenditure levels, the sum of weights of the individual items of food, fuel and light, and clothing and housing is 100 (percent), while it is less than 100 in the miscellaneous group. There is therefore complete coverage in all the groups except miscellaneous. It should be pointed out that it is hardly possible to secure complete coverage in the miscellaneous group in the computation of the price index. Purchase of assets, giving donations, advancement of loans, and expenses on litigations, etc., are some of the expenditure items under the miscellaneous group. Many of these expenditures may not contribute directly to the cost of living of the given class of families. Even if some of the items could, by some stretch of argument, be taken as contributing to living costs, it might not be possible to include them in the construction of the index because of the following reason: While it may be possible to determine the proportion of expenditure on such items, thus providing the weights, it may not be possible to secure the price relatives for such items.

The weights for the miscellaneous group add up to 68.74, 71.74, 69.75, 66.42, and 56.85% in the five expenditure levels, respectively. There is thus an average shortage of about 33%.

Complete coverage is usually securable and has been obtained for each of the remaining major groups of consumption. We should clearly understand here what we mean by complete coverage. When we say that the food group has been completely covered, we do not mean that all items of food that might have been consumed have been included, because in practice it is not possible to do so. Instead, the following has been done: Food has been divided under different heads, such as "cereals," "vegetables," "fish," "meat," etc. There are 25 such heads

comprising total food, as can be seen in Table 1.1. All possible kinds of food are included in these 25 categories (heads or
strata). By stating that complete coverage for food has been
secured, we mean that all possible kinds of food have been included in the construction.

Next comes the question as to how each head (or stratum)
has been covered. In Table 1.5, 51 items were priced to determine the price of a composite commodity, leafy vegetables. The
fact that 51 items were priced does not mean that all kinds of
leafy vegetables that might have been consumed were priced.
Many items might have been left out. If all the remaining items
were priced, the average price of leafy vegetables would not,
perhaps, have differed substantially from the average price of
these 51 items only. The price relative of 51 items would then
be representative of the composite commodity as a whole. The
product of this price relative and the corresponding weight
would thus account for the total cost on this composite commodity. It can thus be said that full account has been taken of
the contribution made by leafy vegetables, although all the subitems might not have been priced (see Chapter 5).

It is thus seen that in securing the complete coverage of
food, food has, in the first place, been divided under different heads (strata), and then each head has been covered with
representative subitems. The implication of complete coverage
here is therefore the same as is understood in the context of
"stratified sampling," where samples are taken from each stratum.

1.13. PRICE COLLECTION

Accuracy in price collection determines the accuracy of
the index. Therefore, the organizational setup of the price-
collecting agents has to be carefully planned.

An examination of the items to be priced may reveal that
there are some items whose prices are not likely to vary within one month, one quarter, or even one year. There should
therefore be no necessity for collecting the price quotations
for such items more frequently than once a month, once a quarter,
or once a year, as the case may be.

In this text, no indication has been given of the number
of markets or "outlets" within a market that may have to be
selected for price collection, or of the bulk of price quotations that may have to be collected for representative averages.
Decisions on these points have to be made from sampling studies
(see Chapter 5). The requirements may vary according to local
conditions.

1.14. FAMILY BUDGET INQUIRY (CONSUMER EXPENDITURE SURVEY)

It has already been pointed out (Sec. 1.7) that weights are
obtained from a family budget inquiry. But the determination of
weights may not be the only objective of a family budget inquiry.
The main objective is the study of family economy in general.
In fact, the study of family budgets is fascinating by itself
(the subject, however, is too comprehensive to be discussed
within the limited scope of this text).

A brief indication will be given here of the way in which
the information available from a family budget inquiry can be
used in the study of family economy. Budgets provide data for
demand analysis, the application of which is very wide indeed.
How is demand influenced by a rise in the income level or the
price level? Does demand for food articles remain the same with
a fall in the income level? How is consumption of luxury goods
influenced by an increase in income? These are only a few of
the questions that might be answered by an objective analysis

of the budget data. Besides providing material for such studies,
the budgets also furnish statistics of general interest. For
example, studies on the joint family system, which is still
prevalent in some Asiatic countries, investigations into per
capita consumption, and an age scale of consumption are only a
few of the topics of interest in this context.

1.15. HOUSING GROUP

The housing group deserves special mention, because difficulties are often faced in determining the individual price relatives in this group. Rent, taxes, and repairs form the three
components of the housing group. House rent or taxes do not,
in general, change frequently. The cost on account of these
two items is therefore expected to remain unaltered over a certain period of time. Cost on account of house repairs may, however, vary more often than that of the other two items. In some
places, prices of building materials are collected for price
relatives under house repairs. But the price relatives for house
rent or taxes cannot be secured so easily. Although there may
not be any change in the cost on account of house rent or taxes
within a short period, it is necessary, nonetheless, to calculate the relatives at least once to begin with, and for this
purpose a survey of housing conditions might be necessary. A
questionnaire for such a survey should have provision for details of floor space, house rent, taxes, etc. Information on
these points should be available for both the base period and
the period compared.

A simple suggestion is indicated below for utilizing such
information in calculating the required price relative for
rent. All the sampled houses may not be rented. The houses
that are rented may be separated from those that are not. The

housing spaces for these two categories of houses taken together
are the total housing space. Let

    S be the total housing space

    s be the total rented space

    r be the total rent for the rented space

    M be the total number of members occupying the housing
       space and

    μ be the average size of family

The space needed per member (per capita space) can be calculated from the total available space, rented and nonrented.
This is S/M. If this figure is multiplied by the average family size, space needed per family on the average is given by
$S\mu/M$. If this is multiplied by the rent per unit space, which
is r/s, the rent per family is given by $(S/M)(\mu r/s)$.

The rent can be calculated as above for both the base
period and the period compared, and the relative can be calculated from these two rents.

The M and μ may remain substantially the same for the
two periods and may not therefore affect the calculation of the
relative, since these parameters cancel out, being the same in
the numerator and the denominator of the required relative.
The relative for taxes may be similarly computed.

The above is just a simple, workable suggestion that may
be acceptable when separate indexes are not required for those
families that own houses and for those that do not. In practice, the problem may be more difficult than visualized here
and would then be tackled on an ad hoc basis depending on the
requirements and the complexities of the situation.

Chapter 2

THE CHAIN INDEX, THE TESTS BASIC IN THE THEORY
OF INDEX NUMBERS, AND OTHER THEORETICAL CONSIDERATIONS

2.1. THE CHAIN INDEX

Computation of index numbers over distant periods of time
by any of the formulas in Chapter 1 has a limitation because
of the time interval. If the two periods compared are consecutive or close, comparison of the living costs between such
periods is expected to be more realistic than between two periods separated by a long interval. This happens because the
pattern of consumption (and therefore the weights) might be
widely divergent during two distant periods; the pattern might
not ordinarily differ much from one period to a proximate period unless, of course, abnormal circumstances intervene.

The limitation of comparison between any two periods separated by an interval of periods can be minimized if the comparison is made to consist of a chain of comparisons, each between two consecutive periods and each time on a changed base.
The method of constructing index numbers with the base changed
from period to period as herein suggested is known as the <u>chain
method</u> as against the <u>fixed-base</u> <u>method</u>, where the base remains
fixed.

Let I_{01} be an index in which the period 1 is compared
with the period 0. Then each of the indexes I_{01}, I_{02}, ..., I_{0n},
I_{12}, I_{13}, ..., I_{1n} has a distinct meaning. The first subscript
of the index refers to the base, and the second refers to the
period compared. Thus, I_{02} means an index number for the period 2 with reference to the base 0. In general, I_{jk} stands
for the index number for the period k compared to the base j.

The series I_{01}, I_{12}, I_{23}, ..., $I_{k-1,k}$ constitutes what
can be called a <u>chain</u> <u>of</u> <u>indexes</u>. The period compared in one
index becomes the base in the succeeding index. Each of these
indexes can be regarded as a link in the chain. The length of
the chain $I_{01}I_{12}$ is from 0 to 2. The end point 1 of the first
link I_{01} is, as it were, forged with the starting point of the
second link, and the resultant chain is obtained as I_{02}, which
is of length $(0,2)$. This relationship can be formalized as
$I_{01}I_{12} = \bar{I}_{02}$, where $\bar{I}_{02}$ denotes the chain index for the period 2 referred to the period 0. A bar is placed above I_{02}
to distinguish it from I_{02}. The equals sign between $I_{01}I_{12}$
and $\bar{I}_{02}$ means that the product of the indexes I_{01} and I_{12}
is the chain index for the period 2 compared to the period 0.
Similarly, the index for the period t compared to the period
0 is $\bar{I}_{0t} = I_{01}I_{12} \cdots I_{t-1,t}$.

In general, $\bar{I}_{j1}\bar{I}_{1k} = \bar{I}_{jk}$, where $\bar{I}_{j1}$ and $\bar{I}_{1k}$ are themselves chain indexes. This extension follows immediately from
the above definition of the chain index. The relationship is
obvious when $\bar{I}_{j1}\bar{I}_{1k}$ and $\bar{I}_{jk}$ are expressed in terms of the
original indexes.

2.2. GENERALIZED DEFINITION OF CHAIN INDEX

The generalized definition [32] of chain index is given
by

$$\bar{I}_{st} = \frac{I_{01} \, I_{12} \, \cdots \, I_{t-1,t}}{I_{01} \, I_{12} \, \cdots \, I_{s-1,s}} \tag{2.1}$$

where $\bar{I}_{st}$ indicates the index for the period t compared to the period s. It can be easily verified that this generalized definition is consistent with the definition given in Sec. 2.1, where the first subscript s of $\bar{I}_{st}$ was, by implication, taken as less than the second subscript t.

When $s < t$, the chain index $\bar{I}_{st}$ given in (2.1) reduces to

$$\bar{I}_{st} = I_{s,s+1} I_{s+1,s+2} \, \cdots \, I_{t-1,t}$$

obtained by cancelling $I_{01} \, I_{12} \, \cdots \, I_{s-1,s}$ from the numerator and the denominator of (2.1). The above form of $\bar{I}_{st}$ agrees with the form given by the definition of Sec. 2.1.

When $s > t$, we have, by the definition of Sec. 2.1,

$$I_{01} I_{12} \, \cdots \, I_{t-1,t} \quad \bar{I}_{ts} = \bar{I}_{0s}$$

or

$$\bar{I}_{0t} \bar{I}_{ts} = \bar{I}_{0s}$$

$$\therefore \; \bar{I}_{ts} = \frac{\bar{I}_{0s}}{\bar{I}_{0t}}$$

Definition (2.1) also gives the above form for $\bar{I}_{ts}$.

In both the above verifications, the first subscript of the chain index is taken as less than the second subscript, as implied in the definition of Sec. 2.1. But the generalized definition works irrespective of whether the first subscript is less than, equal to, or greater than the second subscript. When $s > t$ in $\bar{I}_{st}$, $\bar{I}_{st}$ is interpreted as the reciprocal of $\bar{I}_{ts}$ in terms of the definition of Sec. 2.1, as shown below.

By definition (2.1),

$$\bar{I}_{st} = \frac{\bar{I}_{0t}}{\bar{I}_{0s}} \quad \text{and} \quad \bar{I}_{ts} = \frac{\bar{I}_{0s}}{\bar{I}_{0t}}$$

Multiplying together the above two, we get

$$\bar{I}_{st}\bar{I}_{ts} = 1 \tag{2.2}$$

Hence,

$$\bar{I}_{st} = \frac{1}{\bar{I}_{ts}}$$

The above means that the chain index from s to t, and back from t to s, gives 1. This, in symbols, means that $\bar{I}_{ss} = 1$. Hence, $\bar{I}_{00}$ can be taken as equal to 1 (see Sec. 2.5).

If s and t are taken as the consecutive periods 0 and 1, the chain index $\bar{I}_{01}$ reduces by definition to

$$\bar{I}_{01} = \frac{I_{01}}{I_{00}} = \frac{I_{01}}{1} = I_{01}$$

This follows from the assumption that $I_{00} = 1$ (see Sec. 2.5). Again,

$$\bar{I}_{12} = \frac{I_{01}I_{12}}{I_{01}} = I_{12}$$

Hence, in the case of consecutive periods, we have

$$\bar{I}_{01} = I_{01}, \quad \bar{I}_{12} = I_{12}, \quad \text{etc.}$$

Also, by (2.2),

$$\bar{I}_{01}\bar{I}_{10} = 1$$

2.3.   COMPARISON OF THE CHAIN AND THE FIXED-BASE INDEXES

The difference between the chain method and the fixed base method in constructing indexes is explained in this section through different formulas.

The fixed-weight formula for the price index is known as

$$100 \; \frac{\Sigma \; p_1 q_a}{\Sigma \; p_0 q_a}$$

In this formula, the weights are fixed. That is, whatever the period is, q_a represents the quantity consumed in the period.

Thus, the index I_{0k} by the fixed-base method (with the fixed-weight formula) is, omitting the factor 100,

$$\frac{\Sigma \; p_k q_a}{\Sigma \; p_0 q_a}$$

The same price index by the chain method is given by the product $I_{01} I_{12} I_{23} \cdots I_{k-1,k}$. That is,

$$\bar{I}_{0k} = \frac{\Sigma \; p_1 q_a}{\Sigma \; p_0 q_a} \frac{\Sigma \; p_2 q_a}{\Sigma \; p_1 q_a} \frac{\Sigma \; p_3 q_a}{\Sigma \; p_2 q_a} \cdots \frac{\Sigma \; p_k q_a}{\Sigma \; p_{k-1} q_a}$$

When the numerator of a link is cancelled with the denominator of the succeeding one, $\bar{I}_{0k}$ is given by $\Sigma \; p_k q_a / \Sigma \; p_0 q_a$, which is the same as I_{0k}, i.e., the index by the fixed-base method. It is thus seen that, with the fixed-weight formula, the index by the fixed-base method and that by the chain method give algebraically identical results. In symbols, it means that the fixed-weight formula satisfies the equivalence

$$I_{0k} = \bar{I}_{0k} \quad (= I_{01} I_{12} \cdots I_{k-1,k})$$

or the relationship

$$I_{01}I_{12} \cdots I_{k-1,k} = I_{0k}$$

Let us now adopt the base-weighted formula of Laspeyres for computating the chain index for the period k compared to the base O. Using the same notation and omitting 100 from the numerator, we have

$$I_{0k} = \frac{\Sigma \, p_k q_0}{\Sigma \, p_0 q_0}$$

Again,

$$\bar{I}_{0k} = \frac{\Sigma \, p_1 q_0}{\Sigma \, p_0 q_0} \frac{\Sigma \, p_2 q_1}{\Sigma \, p_1 q_1} \frac{\Sigma \, p_3 q_2}{\Sigma \, p_2 q_2} \cdots \frac{\Sigma \, p_k q_{k-1}}{\Sigma \, p_{k-1} q_{k-1}}$$

We see from the above that $I_{0k} \neq \bar{I}_{0k}$ with Laspeyres' formula. Thus, with Laspeyres' formula, the result obtained by the <u>fixed-base method</u> is not algebraically the same as that given by the chain method.

Of the fixed-base method and the chain method, the latter may be preferred on theoretical grounds. In the chain method, the base changes in every link. Each link makes a comparison between two consecutive periods. The chain is thus the resultant of a series of comparisons, each between two consecutive periods. The chain method thus eliminates the limitation involved in the comparison between two distant periods. It should be realized, however, that computation is much more laborious in the chain method than in the fixed-base method. Additional work in every period is involved in securing the weights. The fixed-base method does not involve such additional labor. From the viewpoint of ease of calculation, the fixed-base method is preferable. The fixed-base method may therefore be recommended when a series of index numbers is needed as a matter of administrative routine. In precision studies, however, the chain method may be preferred, because there is no point in sacrificing precision in the interest of simplicity.

2.4.   INDEX NUMBERS ON A SHIFTED BASE WITHOUT CHANGING THE WEIGHTS

At an intermediate period during the run of a series of index numbers, it might be necessary to start a new series on a base different from the one from which the series started.   To be specific, let us suppose that a series is in progress with November 1950 as the base and that, for the purpose of some specific study, it is necessary to start a series with July 1953 as the base.   The correct procedure is to find new weights operative at the new base period and to construct index numbers as usual.   But the determination of new weights may not be feasible or considered necessary.   The following suggestion can be accepted in such a situation.   The index number for the period July 1953, calculated in the usual manner with November 1950 as the base, can be taken as 100, and the succeeding index numbers with the same base (November 1950) can be transformed to this scale, i.e., expressed in terms of the index number for July 1953 taken as 100.   What is proposed here can be expressed in symbols as follows:

Let November 1950 be denoted as the period 0 and July 1953 as the period s.   Then, in accordance with the notations explained before, the index number for the period s compared to the base 0 can be written as I_{0s}.   Let there be another period t (say, September 1953) following the period s.   Then I_{0t} is the index for the period t compared to the base 0.   Index numbers are now shown with s as the base.   That is, we require I_{st}.   According to this suggestion, I_{st} can be calculated as $100 I_{0t}/I_{0s}$.   That is we are hereby accepting the equality (omitting 100)

$$I_{0t} = I_{0s} I_{st} \tag{2.3}$$

Such an equivalence is acceptable if the index is calculated by the chain method.   However, as we have seen, this equivalence

holds good when the weights remain constant, that is, when the
fixed-weight formula is used for the index.

Laspeyres' base-weighted formula may not lead to any appre-
ciable difference within a short period. (See Appendix C for
the choice of the conversion factor. The period s is called
the conversion base.)

2.5.   TESTS TO JUDGE THE MERIT OF AN INDEX NUMBER FORMULA

We apply certain tests (most of which are those of Irving
Fisher [30]) to judge the merit of an index number formula. A
discussion of these tests is essential, because they are basic
in the theory of index numbers.

The Identity Test. The test implies that I_{ss} should be
equal to 1. In words, it means that the index for a period
compared to the same period is 1 (or 100). The name itself
signifies the implication. It can be easily verified and Laspeyres' formula, Paasche's formula, and the ideal formula of
Irving Fisher all meet this test. For instance, with Laspeyres'
formula,

$$I_{st} = \frac{\Sigma\, p_t q_s}{\Sigma\, p_s q_s}$$

If s is substituted for t, we get $I_{ss} = 1$.

Whatever the primary index number formula with which the
chain index is constructed, the chain index satisfies the identity test, since we already know that $\bar{I}_{ss} = 1$ (see Sec. 2.2).

The Time Reversal Test (point reversal test). The time
reversal test requires that the formula satisfying it work both
ways in time, forward and backward, and that, when it is made
to work both ways, reciprocal results be obtained. If a formula

gives the index for a given period t as twice that in the base period s, that is, if $I_{st} = 2$, the formula, when reversed in time, should give the index for the period s compared to the period t, as $1/2$. This implication is formalized in notation as $I_{st}I_{ts} = 1$.

Putting $t = s$ in this relationship, we get $I_{ss}^2 = 1$. Taking its square root, and remembering that an index can be only real and positive, we get $I_{ss} = 1$. This implies fulfillment of the identity test. Thus, when the time reversal test is satisfied, the condition of the identity test is automatically fulfilled.

As we noticed before, the chain index satisfies the time reversal test, since $\bar{I}_{st}\bar{I}_{ts} = 1$.

Laspeyres' formula does not pass the time reversal test.

The cost of living index for the given period t compared to the base period s is $\Sigma p_t q_s / \Sigma p_s q_s$. If there is now a reversal in time, that is, if the index is required for the period s compared to the period t, the formula takes the form $\Sigma p_s q_t / \Sigma p_t q_t$. The implication of the test is that the product of $\Sigma p_t q_s / \Sigma p_s q_s$ and $\Sigma p_s q_t / \Sigma p_t q_t$ should be equal to unity. It can be seen, however, that the product is not equal to 1.

Paasche's formula does not satisfy this test either.

Taking the ideal formula of Irving Fisher in the form

$$\left(\frac{\Sigma p_t q_s}{\Sigma p_s q_s} \ \frac{\Sigma p_t q_t}{\Sigma p_s q_t} \right)^{1/2}$$

and reversing it in time, i.e., by changing the subscripts s and t, we get

$$\left(\frac{\Sigma p_s q_t}{\Sigma p_t q_t} \ \frac{\Sigma p_s q_s}{\Sigma p_t q_s} \right)^{1/2}$$

EDINBURGH UNIVERSITY LIBRARY
WITHDRAWN

The product of these two is equal to 1. The ideal formula therefore satisfies this test.

In the case of a formula not meeting this test, an error is
made in the index. The difference from 1 is taken as a measure
of the error. The error is joint, since it is contributed to
jointly by the forward and backward applications of the formula.
Because the fulfillment of the test implies that $I_{st}I_{ts} = 1$,
the error from failure to satisfy the time reversal test can be
measured by $I_{st}I_{ts} - 1$.

The Factor Reversal Test. It is mentioned in Chapter 1
that by an interchange of p and q [31] the formula for price
index changes to one for quantity index. The same type of formula is utilized for both purposes. The quality of this joint
performance is judged by the factor reversal test. A formula
is said to have satisfied the factor reversal test if the product of the price and quantity indexes given by the formula is
identically equal to the value index. Let us illustrate this
test with reference to Laspeyres' formula. By this formula,

$$I_{st}(\text{price}) \equiv P_{st} = \frac{\Sigma\, p_t q_s}{\Sigma\, p_s q_s}$$

By the same formula, $I_{st}(\text{quantity}) \equiv Q_{st}$ is obtained, by an
interchange of p and q, as $\Sigma\, q_t p_s / \Sigma\, q_s p_s$. The values (total
costs) in the periods s and t are $\Sigma\, p_s q_s$ and $\Sigma\, p_t q_t$,
respectively. The value index (i.e., relative cost) is
$\Sigma\, p_t q_t / \Sigma\, p_s q_s$ $(= V_{st})$. The fulfillment of the test implies
that $P_{st} Q_{st}$ should be equal to V_{st}. That is, the product of
$\Sigma\, p_t q_s / \Sigma\, p_s q_s$ and $\Sigma\, q_t p_s / \Sigma\, q_s p_s$ should be equal to
$\Sigma\, p_t q_t / \Sigma\, p_s q_s$. But this is not satisfied. Hence, Laspeyres'
formula does not satisfy the factor reversal test.

However, whatever the type of formula (the formulas discussed in Sec. 1.4) with which the index is calculated, the test is satisfied if only one commodity is involved in the construction of the index. The case of one commodity, although trivial, is mentioned here as an illustration.

It has been shown above that the factor reversal test is not satisfied by Laspeyres' formula. Nor does Paasche's formula pass this test. Let us now apply the test to the ideal formula. In this case, we have

$$P_{st} \equiv I_{st} = \left(\frac{\Sigma\, p_t q_s}{\Sigma\, p_s q_s} \, \frac{\Sigma\, p_t q_t}{\Sigma\, p_s q_t} \right)^{1/2}$$

If p and q are interchanged, the corresponding formula for quantity index is given by

$$\left(\frac{\Sigma\, q_t p_s}{\Sigma\, q_s p_s} \, \frac{\Sigma\, q_t p_t}{\Sigma\, q_s p_t} \right)^{1/2}$$

The product of these two is equal to $\Sigma\, p_t q_t / \Sigma\, p_s q_s$. Thus, the factor reversal test is satisfied by this formula.

When this test is not satisfied, an error is made, and it is joint, because the error is contributed to jointly by the price index and the quantity index. In symbols, the magnitude of this error is given by $P_{st} Q_{st} - V_{st}$ or by $(P_{st} Q_{st}/V_{st}) - 1$ [30,50].

The Circular Test. The circular test requires that we have

$$I_{21} I_{1s} = I_{2s} \qquad (2.4)$$

where 1, 2, and s are any three periods. Putting $s = 1$ in (2.4), we have $I_{21} I_{11} = I_{21}$. Hence, $I_{11} = 1$. This means that fulfillment of the circular test entails fulfillment of the identity test. Again, putting $s = 2$ in (2.4), we have

$I_{21}I_{12} = I_{22} = 1$. That is, fulfillment of the circular test
also entails fulfillment of the time reversal test.

Let us suppose that the circular test is satisfied. Then,
writing 0 for 2 in (2.4), we get

$$I_{01}I_{1s} = I_{0s} \qquad\qquad (2.5)$$

Now, putting s = 2 in (2.5) and multiplying both sides
by I_{20}, we have

$$I_{01}I_{12}I_{20} = I_{02}I_{20} = 1$$

($\because$ the time reversal test is satisfied), i.e., $I_{01}I_{12}I_{20} = 1$.
Again, let $I_{12}I_{23} = I_{13}$. Then, $I_{01}I_{12}I_{23} = I_{01}I_{13} = I_{03}$.
Since $I_{03}I_{30} = 1$, we have $I_{01}I_{12}I_{23}I_{30} = 1$.

With extension to more periods, the circular test can be
generalized as satisfying the condition

$$I_{01}I_{12} \cdots I_{k-1,k}I_{k,0} = 1 \qquad\qquad (2.6)$$

From (2.6) it is clear that the circular test can be regarded as an extension of the time reversal test. The time reversal test implies that $I_{0k}I_{k0}$ should be equal to 1. The
test involves only two periods, whereas the circular test involves more than two periods. The test is called circular because there is a circularity in the series of the indexes involved in the test, as indicated by (2.6). The series of the
indexes starts from the period 0 and comes back to the period 0
through I_{k0}, completing what can be called a circle. (The
amount by which the left-hand side of (2.6) falls short of 1 is
called the circular gap.)

It is easy to verify that the circular test is not satisfied by Laspeyres', Paasche's, or Fisher's ideal formula but is
satisfied by the fixed-weight formula. It has been shown that
the chain index meets the time reversal test, whatever the

primary formula with which the chain index is computed. That
is, it was shown in Sec. 2.2 that $\bar{I}_{st}\bar{I}_{ts} = 1$. It will now be
demonstrated that the circular test is also satisfied by the
chain index. This follows from the fact that the chain index
$\bar{I}_{2s}$ is equal to $\bar{I}_{21}\bar{I}_{1s}$. More explicitly, by definition the
chain index $\bar{I}_{st}$ is given by

$$\bar{I}_{st} = I_{s,s+1}I_{s+1,s+2} \cdots I_{t-1,t} \qquad (2.7)$$

where the primary indexes $I_{s,s+1}$, $I_{s+1,s+2}$, $\ldots$, $I_{t-1,t}$ have
been constructed by any given formula. Each of the indexes is
for consecutive periods. Hence, as shown in Sec. 2.2, $\bar{I}_{s,s+1} =$
$I_{s,s+1}$; $\bar{I}_{s+1,s+2} = I_{s+1,s+2}$; and so on. We therefore get

$$\bar{I}_{st} = \bar{I}_{s,s+1}\bar{I}_{s+1,s+2} \cdots \bar{I}_{t-1,t}$$

or

$$\bar{I}_{st}\bar{I}_{ts} = 1 = \bar{I}_{s,s+1}\bar{I}_{s+1,s+2} \cdots \bar{I}_{t-1,t}\bar{I}_{t,s}$$

that is,

$$\bar{I}_{s,s+1}\bar{I}_{s+1,s+2} \cdots \bar{I}_{t-1,t}\bar{I}_{t,s} = 1 \qquad (2.8)$$

In general, we have

$$\bar{I}_{0p}\bar{I}_{pn}\bar{I}_{nm} \cdots \bar{I}_{tk} = I_{01}I_{12} \cdots I_{p-1,p}I_{p,p+1} \cdots I_{n-1,n}$$
$$\cdots I_{t,t+1} \cdots I_{k-1,k} \qquad (2.9)$$

The above equality follows when each chain index on the left-
hand side is expressed in terms of the primary indexes. It is
assumed here that $p < n < m \ldots < k$. By definition, the right-
hand side of (2.9) is equal to $\bar{I}_{0k}$. Hence, $\bar{I}_{0p}\bar{I}_{pn}\bar{I}_{nm} \cdots \bar{I}_{tk}$
$= \bar{I}_{0k}$ or $\bar{I}_{0p}\bar{I}_{pn}\bar{I}_{nm} \cdots \bar{I}_{tk}\bar{I}_{k0} = \bar{I}_{0k}\bar{I}_{k0} = 1$. This is more
general than (2.8) in the sense that in (2.8) each of the chain

indexes is between consecutive periods, whereas here each index
is between any two periods.

The Base Test. Let R_{21} denote the ratio of two indexes,
I_{2s} and I_{1s}, where 1, 2, and s are any three arbitrary periods of time. The base test requires that R_{21}, that is,
I_{2s}/I_{1s} be independent of s. In other words, whatever the
third period s through which the comparison is made between
the periods 2 and 1, R_{21} remains unaffected.

The circular test implies that $I_{21} = I_{2s}/I_{1s}$. The circular test is therefore more general than the base test, because
it means that R_{21} is not only independent of s, but is also
equal to I_{21}. Hence, the fulfillment of the circular test entails the fulfillment of the base test. The converse is not
true in general. The converse is true if, along with the fulfillment of the base test by any primary index formula, the
identity test is also satisfied. If s is put equal to 1, we
get I_{21}/I_{11} for R_{21}. Since the identity test is satisfied
by the primary index formula, $I_{11} = 1$. Hence, R_{21} is the same
as I_{21}. That is, the circular test is fulfilled.

If, however, R_{21} is treated as a derived index (by derived
index we mean an index derived from the primary indexes just as
a chain index is), R_{21} will pass both the identity and the time
reversal tests. Substituting 1 for 2, we get $R_{11} = I_{1s}/I_{1s} = 1$.
Hence, the identity test is satisfied. Again,

$$R_{21}R_{12} = (I_{2s}/I_{1s})(I_{1s}/I_{2s}) = 1$$

That is, the time reversal test is satisfied.

The Commensurability Test. This test implies that a change
in the unit of measurement does not affect the index number [31].
If for q we write q/λ and for p we write λp, as we should
in case we want to keep the outlay the same, the index number
I_{01} should remain unchanged whatever the value of λ.

The Determinateness Test. "The test requires that the index number shall not be rendered zero, infinite, or indeterminate by an individual price or quantity becoming zero" [31].

The Proportionality Test. "If all the individual prices have changed into the same proportion from O to 1, I_{01} shall be equal to the common factor of proportionality" [31].

For a detailed discussion of these tests, see the article by R. Frisch [31].

To what extent these tests are helpful in finding the "best index," or the "true index" is briefly discussed in the preliminary remarks of Sec. 4.1.

2.6. THE STATUS OF LASPEYRES' AND PAASCHE'S FORMULAS

We begin this section with the following observation. The superiority of one formula over another need not solely be judged on the basis of tests. A formula has to be economically meaningful. The fact that the fixed-weight formula satisfies the circular test, which is not satisfied by Fisher's ideal formula, does not necessarily lead to the conclusion that the fixed-weight formula is better than the ideal formula. One objection is that the usefulness of the circular test itself may be questioned. An argument against its usefulness is that I_{k0} is a retrograde step in time which cannot always be taken; difficulties increase when O is far behind k. Although Laspeyres' and Paasche's formulas fail to pass the time reversal, the factor reversal, and the circular tests, these formulas have other merits.

Laspeyres' and Paasche's formulas have been found to be economically meaningful, because each of these formulas answers a specific question. Laspeyres' formula answers the question: How does the cost of living in the current year compare with the

cost in the base year for the base year goods and services?
Similarly, Paasche's index provides such a comparison on the
basis of the current year's goods and services.

Judging from all considerations, Fisher [30] classified
both Laspeyres' and Paasche's formulas as "very good" and the
ideal formula as "superlative." Formulas (1.7) through (1.9)
also came under "superlative," while the fixed-weight formula
was classified as "fair" [45,50]. The fixed-weight formula
therefore stands last in order of merit. One of the objections
to the fixed-weight formula is that the p-q data are not causally
connected.

In this context, it is relevant to know the relative positions of Laspeyres' (L) and Paasche's (P) formulas with respect to the trends that they would show: L overestimates the
index, whereas P underestimates the index. To provide some
reasoning that they really do so, we can consider the application of L and P to data in the following two situations.
Let the prices p_1 in the given period be higher than p_0, the
prices in the base period. In L ($= \Sigma p_1 q_0 / \Sigma p_0 q_0$), the base
year quantities q_0 are priced by p_0 and p_1, and the ratio
of the aggregate costs is taken as the index. If p_1 is greater
than p_0, there will be a redistribution of expenditure through
the quantities consumed in the period 1, during which the items
of higher price will probably be consumed in lesser quantities
than q_0. But, according to the formula, larger quantities are
actually being priced with higher prices. The numerator in L,
being the sum of the products of the higher prices and the larger
quantities, will tend to be higher than in the actual pattern of
consumption. Thus, L has the tendency to overestimate [45] the
index. Now let P be applied to an opposite situation in which
the prices p_1 are lower than the prices p_0. If p_0 is higher
than p_1, the quantities consumed in the period 0 should, in
the redistribution of expenditure, be lower than the quantities

q_1 consumed in the period 1. By the application of P
$(= \Sigma \ p_1 q_1 / \Sigma \ p_0 q_1)$, therefore, the denominator will be higher
than in the actual pattern of consumption. Thus, P has the
tendency to underestimate the index.

However, it is quite possible that Laspeyres' formula may,
in an actual situation, still report an algebraically lower index [45] than Paasche's formula.

The fact that L overestimates and P underestimates the
index holds good in general irrespective of whether the trend
in price change is upward or downward (see Sec. 4.8).

In the computation of the index, either L or P can be
used. There is nothing to choose between the two; both stand
on equal footing. Both make use of the p-q data that have
causal connection. In light of the remarks made in the pre-
ceding paragraphs, it is clear that an error is introduced in
any case, whether L or P is used. The error decreases with
the closeness of agreement between the indexes by L and P.
The cause of the disagreement between L and P is traceable
to the difference between q_0 and q_1. This disagreement is
less and less as the periods of comparison come closer and
closer. Therefore, if the comparison is made between two consecutive periods, the formula error should be the least. This,
incidentally, is a justification for the use of the chain index.

2.7. COMPONENTS OF ERROR OF AN INDEX

Formula Error. It has been shown above that none of the
main formulas satisfies all the tests. Whatever formula is used,
it has a limitation that introduces an error, which can be called
the formula error. In the discussion on tests, an indication
was given of the measure of error resulting from failure to
satisfy the time reversal and factor reversal tests.

Homogeneity Error. The Σ pq occurring in a formula
stands for the total expenditure on all items. Strictly speak-
ing, an index number is expected to be a comparison of such
total expenditures in two periods. But, in practice, comparison
on the basis of total expenditure is not feasible. Again, the
commodities consumed in the two periods may not remain common.
The common commodities are called binary commodities [50], and
those that are not common are called unique commodities. If
there are unique commodities in the two periods, the total expenditures are not strictly comparable.

Because price relatives are not available for unique commodities, these commodities are not included in the calculation.
The comparison has to be restricted to binary commodities only.
The comparison is thus subject to error. This error is called
homogeneity error. The error is due to the heterogeneity of
the commodities consumed in the two periods. Let N_0 and N_1
be the total numbers of commodities consumed in the periods 0
and 1, respectively, and let N_{01} be the number of binary commodities. The total number of unique commodities in the two
periods is therefore

$$\left(N_1 - N_{01}\right) + \left(N_0 - N_{01}\right) = N_1 + N_0 - 2N_{01}$$

as against the total number of commodities, $N_1 + N_0$. A measure
of heterogeneity can therefore be obtained from the proportion
of the number of unique commodities to the total number of all
commodities. In symbols, this measure is denoted by

$$R = \frac{N_1 + N_0 - 2N_{01}}{N_1 + N_0}$$

The value of R lies between 0 and 1. If $R = 0$, there is
complete homogeneity. To make $R = 0$, the numerator of R
should be zero. That is, there is no unique commodity. Again,
if $R = 1$, there is complete heterogeneity. To make $R = 1$,

the numerator of R should be equal to its denominator, which
implies that all the commodities are unique commodities.

It is probable that the heterogeneity will increase with
distance between the two periods compared. The error on this
account can therefore be minimized if the distance between the
periods is minimized. The error will obviously be the least
when the two periods are consecutive.

It is thus evident that both the homogeneity error and
the formula error can be controlled by taking periods of comparison sufficiently close. These two components of error are
therefore the least when the index is computed by the chain
method because each link in the chain is a comparison between
two consecutive periods.

Sampling Error. In the selection of items to be priced,
sampling is inevitable. There is therefore a sampling error
as well. The questions of sampling and sampling error are discussed at length in Chapter 5.

Part II

PRECISION AND THEORY

Chapter 3

COMPUTATION OF COST OF LIVING INDEX
NUMBERS FOR DIFFERENT AREAS AT ONE POINT OF TIME

3.1.   MEANING OF COST OF LIVING INDEX NUMBERS
FOR DIFFERENT AREAS AT
ONE POINT OF TIME

Methods of compiling cost of living index numbers over time
have been discussed in Part I. Nothing has been said so far
about cost of living index numbers for different areas at one
point of time. The distinction between the two has to be clearly
understood.

When we say that the cost of living index number during
December 1953 in a given city was 95.5 referred to the base
November 1950, we mean that the index number during November
1950 in the city was 100 and that the cost of living has since
gone down to 95.5 in December 1953. On the same base, index
numbers are constructed for different periods of time as a time
series. Therefore, the series of index numbers at different
points of time afford a comparison of the cost of living at
those points of time.

In a similar manner, another series of index numbers can be compiled with November 1950 as the base with respect to another city, say, city A. Let us suppose that the index number during December 1953 was 88.2 in city A. This means that the cost of living in city A decreased from 100 in November 1950 to 88.2 in December 1953.

The cost of living in both the first city and city A was 100 during November 1950, and the two series started independently from this point of time. In each series, the indexes are comparable over time. That is, if the index during January 1954 in the series of the first city were 95.5, the cost of living during December 1953 and January 1954 could be assumed to be the same. Similarly comparable would be any two indexes in the series for city A.

The indexes during November 1950 are taken as 100 in both series. This does not mean that the cost of living was the same in the first city and in city A in November 1950. The cost of living in city A relative to that in the first city might have been different in this period. Similarly, two indexes, one from each of the two time series corresponding to any other point of time, would not be comparable.

The aim of this chapter is to show how index numbers can be constructed for different areas at one point of time to furnish an idea of the relative costliness between different areas.

3.2. COMPUTATION OF COST OF LIVING INDEX NUMBERS FOR DIFFERENT CITIES AT ONE POINT OF TIME

A comparison of the cost of living in a number of cities at a particular point of time may at times be needed. This comparison might be required in relation to the cost of living in a given city. The compilation of such comparative indexes

involves various difficulties which increase with distance between the cities compared. People living in two cities in two
different countries may have widely different consumption habits[*]
and standards of living (explained in Chapter 4). In such a
situation, the solution of the problem can hardly be expected
to be flawless, if possible at all. The task is comparatively
easy when the comparison is to be made between two cities within the same state, that is, between two areas that are sufficiently close together and whose inhabitants have nearly the
same consumption habits.

The computation of such indexes is a matter of research
but, for the purposes of routine practice, two suggestions are
offered here. The cities compared in the analyses below are
within a state. The underlying assumption is that the inhabitants have nearly the same consumption habits. The arguments
advanced are of a general nature and can therefore be applied to
the compilation of such indexes elsewhere under the same assumption.

Suggestion 1. Both Laspeyres' formula $(\Sigma\, p_1 q_0 / \Sigma\, p_0 q_0)$
and Paasche's formula $(\Sigma\, p_1 q_1 / \Sigma\, p_0 q_0)$, which are used in constructing index numbers for cost of living over time, can also
be used in constructing index numbers over different areas.
These two formulas, which can be denoted by L_{01} and P_{01}, reduce, respectively, to the forms

$$L_{01} \equiv \frac{100\, \Sigma\, p_1 q_0}{\Sigma\, p_0 q_0} = \frac{100\, \Sigma\, (p_1/p_0)\, p_0 q_0}{\Sigma\, p_0 q_0} = \frac{\Sigma\, r_i w_i}{\Sigma\, w_i}$$

---

[*]In this connection the reports of the International Labour
Office, Geneva [36], can be studied.

$$P_{01} = \frac{100 \sum p_1 q_1}{\sum p_0 q_1} = \frac{100}{\sum p_0 q_1 / \sum p_1 q_1}$$

$$= \frac{100^2 (\sum p_1 q_1)}{100 \sum (p_0/p_1) p_1 q_1} = \frac{100^2}{\sum r_i' w_i' / \sum w_i'}$$

The prime above r_i and w_i in P_{01} is used to differentiate the price relatives and the weights of P_{01} from those of L_{01}. In L_{01}, the price relatives r_i are the relatives of the prices in the period 1 (the period compared) to those in the period 0 (the base period). The weights w_i relate to the base period. In P_{01} the price relatives r_i' are the relatives of the prices in the base period to those in the period compared, and the weights w_i' are drawn from the period compared. The price ratios involved in r_i and r_i' are reciprocals.

Just as a period is kept fixed as the base period in the indexes over time, a city can be kept fixed as the base city in the indexes over cities. The prices ruling in the base city are treated in the same manner as the base period prices; that is, the price relatives of the prices in the city compared are calculated with reference to the prices in the base city in the same manner as is done in calculating the indexes over time.

If the family budget inquiries are conducted in all the areas or cities to be compared, data would be available to use Paasche's formula (P) as well. In that event, however, it would be preferable to use Fisher's ideal formula (F), as data for using both L and P would be available.

Suggestion 2. The information on expenditure on different items of consumption can be utilized as such for this comparison. The cost can be found per family, per capita (member), or per adult in each city and compared.

Comparison on the basis of the cost per family can be questioned on the grounds that the number of members per family might vary from city to city. It can hence be argued that per capita cost would perhaps serve better as the basis of comparison. But per capita cost, too, is not free from limitations. The difference in the compositions with regard to the number of adults and children per average family in the two cities might result in a difference of cost, apart from the real difference that we want to measure. Judged in this perspective, the cost per adult equivalent might appear to be a better guide than either of the former measures. However, because cost of living is conceptually related to an average family, it would perhaps be preferable to make the comparison on the basis of cost per family.

The expression "adult equivalent" referred to in Suggestion 2 requires an explanation. Generally, a child or a minor consumes less than an adult. If the consumption of an adult is taken as 1, the consumption per member in a lower age group can be expressed as a fraction. If the consumption of a child below 6 years is taken as 0.5, two children taken together are equivalent to one adult. Therefore, 0.5 is the conversion factor. It expresses a child in terms of an adult equivalent. The total members of the families in a city can be reduced to adult equivalents with the help of such conversion factors.

The Lusk scale of conversion, which is sometimes used in such studies, is reproduced below:

Adult male	1.00
Adult female	0.83
Child between 10 and 14	0.83
Child between 6 and 10	0.70
Child under 6	0.50

Incidentally, it is possible to construct the appropriate age scale of consumption from the data compiled in a family budget inquiry. Indeed, it is better to find out the scale of conversion [26] from the available data and use those conversion factors in such studies than to use a scale that might have been obtained for different purposes under different conditions.

The age scale of Lusk applies to the consumption of total food. "Consumption" of clothing also varies from an adult to a child. An age scale could therefore be constructed for the clothing group as well. In addition, the consumption of some items in the miscellaneous group varies according to the age of the consumers. There may also exist a variation in the cost per head from an adult to a child with respect to other major groups. If considerable variation is found to exist, the age scale has to be obtained from family budget studies.

The Lusk scale of conversion may not hold individually for all food items. For instance, application of the scale may not be justified with respect to an item like milk, which may be consumed more by a child than by an adult. But only a small fraction of the total expenditure may go to milk. Therefore, such items of small consumption may not seriously affect the applicability of the scale to total food in general.

Chapter 4

AN INTRODUCTION TO THE CONCEPT OF TRUE INDEX

4.1. PRELIMINARY REMARKS

In Chapter 1, mention was made of seven formulas for constructing cost of living index numbers, while actual computation
was illustrated with reference to Laspeyres' formula. Any one
of the seven could have been used for the purpose. In fact,
many more formulas are known. Each of them was evolved heuris-
tically, and each could be taken as approximating the cost of
living index. The multiplicity of such formulas raised the
question of their relative merits. The development of formal
tests, as explained in Chapter 2, resulted from the attempt to
determine which formulas could be regarded as good, better, or
the best. Irving Fisher tested 134 formulas by those test criteria. Forty-one met the time reversal test or the factor reversal test and 13 out of 41 met both these tests. The ideal
formula of Fisher passed both the time reversal and the factor
reversal tests, but it did not pass the circular test. R. Frisch
[31] showed that no single formula can pass the commensurability,

71

determinateness, and circular tests and observed that "even if
some of the tests are abandoned, the remaining ones do not lead
to a unique formula." Therefore, the formal tests could not
serve as a guide to the best formula.

But the search for a unique formula could not be dampened
by the failure of the tests. The search continued and led to
the fundamental question as to what a cost of living index number should really mean. A precise definition was therefore in
quest, a requirement that the general heuristic approach could
not meet.

The behavior of price movement is an economic phenomenon,
and the consumption of goods is economically connected with
price movement. Therefore, the definition of the measurement
of price level automatically involves the consideration of economic concepts. It is along this line of thinking that the
definition of the index, or rather the definition of the true
index, found its expression in a comparison of utilities derived
from the consumption of goods and services in the periods compared. A. A. Konüs was perhaps the first to start investigations along this line. His original article appeared in 1924
in the _Economic_ _Bulletin_ _of_ _Moscow_.[*] To comprehend his approach,
it is necessary to be familiar with some preliminary economic
concepts. These concepts will be explained before the definition of the true index is taken up.

4.2. UTILITY

Let $U(x)$ be the utility corresponding to the x units
of an owned commodity. Utility $U(x)$ increases in general as
x increases and attains an upper limit. It declines after a

---

[*]For the English version of the article, see ref. [45].

certain stage, the stage of disutility. When that stage is
reached, utility up to the final degree has been obtained.
Marginal utility is characterized by the first derivative dU/dx
of the function U(x). As a derivative, dU/dx stands for the
ratio of change in utility corresponding to a unit change in x
at a given x. In general, dU/dx continually declines in value,
tending toward zero, beyond which there is no further addition
to utility. Therefore, the maximum total utility has been attained when that limiting stage characterized by dU/dx = 0 is
reached.

The concept of utility as explained above is true not only
in the case of one commodity, that is, one variable; it can be
extended to more than one commodity. Let $U = U(x_1, x_2, \ldots, x_n)$
be the utility of consuming the amounts $x_1, x_2, \ldots, x_n$ of n
goods. The function $U(x_1, x_2, \ldots, x_n)$ can be regarded as a
surface on an n-dimensional space called the commodity space.
Every point, given by the ordered set of coordinates $(x_1, x_2, \ldots, x_n)$, in the space represents a particular combination of
the n commodities.

It will be assumed that U is a continuous function and
that its derivatives at least up to the second order exist. The
assumption of continuity implies that it is possible to move
continuously from one point $(x_1, x_2, \ldots, x_n)$ to another point
$(x_1', x_2', \ldots, x_n')$. This assumption appears reasonable when the
consumption is taken as that of an average individual, that is,
when the quantities $x_1, x_2, \ldots, x_n$ are taken as the statistical averages of consumption of a sufficiently homogeneous
group of consumers. The first- and second-order derivatives
are

$$U_i = \frac{\delta U}{\delta x_i}, \quad U_{ij} = \frac{\delta^2 U}{\delta x_i \, \delta x_j}, \quad i, j = 1, 2, \ldots, n \qquad (4.1)$$

The first-order derivative U_i represents the marginal utility of the ith item of the goods, where $i = 1, 2, \ldots, n$. The increment in the utility U can be expressed in differential notation as

$$dU = U_1\ dx_1 + U_2\ dx_2 + \cdots + U_n\ dx_n \qquad (4.2)$$

The total utility is obtained by summing up (i.e., integrating) the differential (4.2). This can be done under certain conditions, but no attempt will be made here to deduce the conditions of integrability [27].

The conditions under which U is a maximum can be found in any textbook on calculus. For U to be a maximum, d^2U must be negative definite. This implies that U is a convex function, convex to the origin.

Let us, for a moment, consider U to be a function only of x_1 and x_2, and let us suppose that there is neither gain nor loss in utility from the consumption of the amounts x_1 and x_2 of the two commodities. Then $dU = U_1\ dx_1 + U_2\ dx_2$ is identically equal to zero. That is, $-dx_2/dx_1 = U_1/U_2$. The ratio $U_1/U_2 = r_{12}$ is called the marginal rate of substitution of x_2 for x_1. This means that, at a given level of consumption, the value of r_{12} is equal to the increased consumption of x_2 necessary to compensate for a given unit reduction of x_1.

4.3. BUDGET EQUATION AND MAXIMIZATION OF UTILITY

If an average individual has a given amount of money to spend on his necessities and freedom in choosing his purchases, he will select a combination of goods that will bring him maximal satisfaction ("want" satisfaction). In other words, given

a certain money income to be spent on necessities in a given
price situation, the individual will try to maximize his utility by a judicious selection of goods. His budget is represented by

$$p_1 x_1 + p_2 x_2 + \cdots + p_n x_n = E \qquad\qquad (4.3)$$

where x_1, x_2, ..., x_n are the amounts of n goods purchased
with the respective prices p_1, p_2, ..., p_n, and E is the
total expenditure. Equation (4.3) is called the budget equation and is referred to as the budget plane. [In fact, Eq.
(4.3) represents an n-1 flat in the commodity space of n dimensions.]

Therefore, when an individual's utility has to be maximized,
it must be maximized subject to the restraint $\Sigma_{i=1}^{n} p_i x_i = E$.
That is, when the total outlay and the prices of the commodities
are given, the x values have to be determined such that utility is maximal. The problem then reduces to maximizing the
function $U = U(x_1, x_2, ..., x_n)$ subject to the condition
$\Sigma_{i=1}^{n} p_i x_i = E$. When U is maximized under this restraint, the
values of the variables x_1, x_2, ..., x_n and of λ_1 are determined by the equations

$$U_1 + \lambda_1 p_1 = 0$$
$$U_2 + \lambda_1 p_2 = 0$$
$$\vdots$$
$$U_n + \lambda_1 p_n = 0$$
$$\sum_{i=1}^{n} p_i x_i = E$$

$$(4.4)$$

where λ_1 is the constant involved in the Lagrangian method of
maximizing a function under a given restraint. From (4.4), we
get

$$\frac{U_1}{p_1} = \frac{U_2}{p_2} = \cdots = \frac{U_n}{p_n} \tag{4.5}$$

Prices here are assumed to be constant, that is, independent of the quantities consumed.

The relations (4.5) are a set of necessary conditions for the maximum to exist. They mean that the marginal utilities of the different commodities are proportional to their prices. The point $(x_1, x_2, \ldots, x_n)$ in the commodity space maximizing the utility under the restraint of the budget equation is known as the equilibrium point.

Conditions (4.5) are also described as the optimum conditions.

4.4. INDIFFERENCE SURFACE

The utility from the consumption of two goods, x_1 and x_2, can be represented by x_3, a coordinate in the third dimension; x_3 can be taken as the height over the plane of x_1 and x_2. A higher utility is represented by a higher value of x_3, that is, a higher ordinate over the plane of x_1 and x_2. The end points of such ordinates describe a surface in three dimensions. The surface can be taken as $U(x_1, x_2) = x_3$, where $U(x_1, x_2)$ stands for the utility. If $x_3 = K = $ constant, we get $U(x_1, x_2) = K$, which defines the locus of the different combinations of the two commodities, owned or consumed, which afford equal utility K to the individual. Each point on this locus is a combination of the goods such that no point is preferred to any other. In other words, the individual is indifferent whether he chooses one combination or the other so far as the utility is concerned, it remaining the same for any of the combinations.

The curve represented by $U(x_1, x_2) = K$ is described as an in-difference curve.

For two commodities, the utility function is delineable in three dimensions, but $U(x_1, x_2) = K$ is a curve in two dimensions.

In general, for n commodities, an indifference surface is defined by the equation

$$U(x_1, x_2, \ldots, x_n) = K$$

When different values are given to K, a set of non-intersecting indifference surfaces is obtained. All such surfaces taken together form an indifference map.

The utility function is sometimes referred to as a choice indicator, or an indicator represented by $I = I(x_1, x_2, \ldots, x_n)$. The function is supposed to increase monotonically as it passes from one indifference surface to another that is preferred to the first.

4.5.   PREFERENCE DIRECTION

The marginal utilities U_i $(i = 1, 2, \ldots, n)$ can be regarded as the n coordinates of an $\underline{n}$ vector in the direction of the infinitesimal vector $(dx_1, dx_2, \ldots, dx_n)$. Such a vector is called a gradient and is written as

$$\text{grad } \underline{U} = (U_1, U_2, \ldots, U_n)$$

Since the direction cosines of the normal to the plane (hyperplane or $(n-1)$-flat) tangent to the indifference surface are proportional to $(U_1, U_2, \ldots, U_n)$, grad $\underline{U}$ has the direction of the normal and points to the direction of the maximal change of utility. (Any standard text can be consulted for the

derivation of this result.) This direction is called the preference direction. The line drawn through the successive points
of an indifference map in this direction is called a preference
line. All such lines obtained from all points of the indifference map form the preference map.

In Fig. 4.1, the lines AB and CD are the preference
lines. The preference map is defined by the system of the following differential equations:

$$\frac{dx_1}{U_1} = \frac{dx_2}{U_2} = \cdots = \frac{dx_n}{U_n}$$

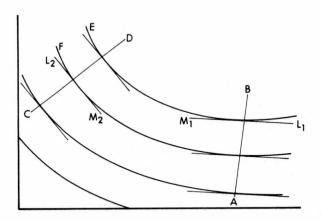

FIG. 4.1. Indifference Map Showing Indifference Curves
(E), (F). Preference Lines (AB, CD) and Budget Lines (L_1M_1)
and (L_2M_2).

4.6.   ENGEL CURVES AND THEIR CONNECTION WITH THE UTILITY FUNCTION

On the assumption that quantities purchased depend entirely on the level of money income, the n quantities purchased can be expressed in notations of mathematical functions as

$$x_1 = f_1(I),\quad x_2 = f_2(I),\quad \ldots,\quad x_n = f_n(I) \tag{4.6}$$

where I represents the money income and can be considered as a variable. This money income can be taken, for all practical purposes, as the actual expenditure incurred on the commodities. Each value of I corresponds to a point $(x_1, x_2, \ldots, x_n)$. As I is made to vary, a locus is obtained. There are n relationships in (4.6), each dependent on the variable I. If I is eliminated, the relationships (4.6) reduce to n-1 independent equations. These n-1 equations represent a 1-flat (or a curve) in the n-dimensional commodity space. This curve is called the Engel curve, after the German economist Earnest Engel (1821-1896).

It has been held that each of the above relationships considered as a function of x and I is linear. This assumption of linearity is referred to in economic literature as Engel's law. Subsequent studies have revealed, however, that this assumption is true only to a first approximation at a moderate income level when the commodity consumed refers to necessities such as food and clothing. The form

$$x = a - be^{-\mu I} \tag{4.7}$$

where a, b, and μ are constants and $b < a$, has been suggested as a realistic approximation to Engel curves within the class of necessities. Expanding $e^{-\mu I}$ in (4.7), we get

$$x = a - b\left(1 - \mu I + \frac{\mu^2 I^2}{2!} \cdots\right) \tag{4.8}$$

If I is assumed to be sufficiently small, I^2 and higher powers
of I can be ignored. Equation (4.8) then reduces to

$$x = a - b + \mu bI \qquad\qquad (4.9)$$

which is linear in x and I. Again, when I is larger and
larger, $e^{-\mu I}$ approaches zero. Hence, (4.7) reduces to x = a.
This shows that however large the income, the quantity consumed
does not exceed a certain limit. This conclusion is in keeping
with reality. That is, however large the income, the purchase
of a necessary article, say, an item of food, does not exceed
a certain limit.

In Sec. 4.5, the concept of a preference line or a preference direction is explained. A preference line meets an indicator at a point where the budget plane (or the flat) is tangent
to the indicator (surface), and the preference line is normal
to the budget plane at the point.

The budget plane defines a price situation. If, in the
same price situation, a higher expenditure is incurred on the
quantities, the quantities refer to an indicator that is preferred to the first. This is true by virtue of the monotonic
property of the indicator. That is, if the prices are allowed
to remain constant and the expenditure is allowed to vary, different budget planes tangent to the different indicators are
obtained. The points of contact are points on the preference
line.

Equations (4.6) give different points in the commodity
space, which vary with expenditure. These points lie on the
different indicators and are the points of contact of the different budget planes with the different indicators to which the
budget planes are tangent. The points therefore lie on the
preference line. As the prices remain the same, the budget
plane moves parallel to itself, remaining tangent to the different indicators, each of which corresponds to an expenditure

level. Hence, Eqs. (4.6) show the preference direction in terms
of the variable I. Much about the form of the utility surface
can therefore be learned from Engle curves, that is, from Eqs.
(4.6). (Students of econometrics may, in the first instance,
refer to the textbook on econometrics by H.T. Davis [27] or to
any similar text and then read the paper by Wald [65] on the
subject.)

4.7. MEANING OF TRUE INDEX

An indifference surface corresponds to a certain scale of
preference of consumption. This scale of preference varies
with the standard of living, which has been defined as the general status of want satisfaction. Therefore, each standard of
living corresponds to a scale of preference or an indifference
surface. The same standard of living is then reached by the
various combinations of the commodities lying on the same indifference surface. The level of the standard of living can
therefore be considered as analogous to the level of utility
to which the utility function is equated to obtain the indifference surface.

"If, in the course of two periods of time, the general
status of want satisfaction of the family--or the "standard of
living" of that family--remains constant, then we obtain the
"true index of the cost of living" by dividing the cost of living at one period of time by the cost of living at the other
period" [45]. The true index of the cost of living is therefore the ratio of the costs required to maintain the same standard of living in the two periods compared. The problem of computing the true index thus becomes simple when the standard of
living (or the indifference surface) remains the same in the
two periods. In such a situation, the true index is the ratio

E_1/E_0, where E_1 and E_0 are the expenditures in the two periods given by the budget equations

$$p_1^0 x_1^0 + p_2^0 x_2^0 + \cdots + p_n^0 x_n^0 = E_0$$
$$p_1^1 x_1^1 + p_2^1 x_2^1 + \cdots + p_n^1 x_n^1 = E_1$$

(4.10)

where 0 refers to the base period, and 1 refers to the period of comparison. These two budget planes (flats) are tangent to the indifference surface defining the same standard of living, as shown in Fig. 4.2.

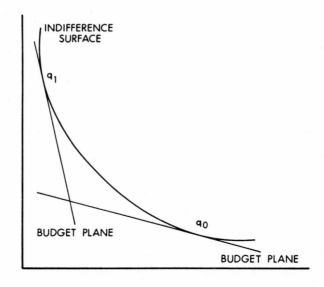

FIG. 4.2.   Indifference surface and budget planes.

It has been mentioned that the utility surface is convex to the origin. It also slopes downward.[*] Figure 4.2 shows

_____

[*]For its proof, see R.G.D. Allen and A.L. Bowley [5].

these properties. The indifference surface is shown for two
commodities only and therefore reduces to a curve. The two
budget lines are tangent to the indifference curve at the points
q_0 and q_1. What is stated here, of course, holds good for n
commodities in general.

It is rarely found in practice that the standard of living
(or the indifference surface) remains the same in the periods
compared. The above diagram portrays an oversimplification of
the problem. Two different budget planes characterized by two
different price situations are tangent to the indifference surfaces at two points, which may not lie on the same indifference
surface. The fact that the standard of living changes creates
difficulty in computing the true index. There have been numerous approaches to approximating the computation of the true index, an account of which is available in a paper by R. Frisch
[32] and in the critical review prepared by H. Staehle [57].

Incidentally, an in-depth study of the problem may reveal
that the true index is an abstract concept that is not capable
of exact measurement. It may in this sense be similar to the
concept of perfect randomness, which can hardly be attained in
practice, however rigorous the procedure of random selection
adopted to ensure randomness.

In actual practice, however, the cost of living index is
computed by the method of aggregates, that is, by the formulas
indicated in Chapter 1. Such aggregative formulas cannot show
the true change in the cost of living as enunciated here. In
the following paragraphs, an account is given of the approach
made by A. A. Konüs.[*] The salient results are indicated below without proofs.

---

[*] The proofs are elegant and can be referred to in the
original paper [45]. It will be helpful if the commentary by
Henry Schultz [55] on the Konüs condition is also studied in
this connection.

4.8. APPROACH MADE BY A. A. KONÜS

Starting with the definition of the standard of living and the postulates of the existence of the utility function and of maximizing utility, the first theorem Konüs proves is the following: "Suppose that a consumer, during a certain period of time, under a given price situation, consumed a combination of goods which determined a certain standard of living. If, in another period of time, at changed prices, the consumer spends a sum of money equal to the cost of the first combination of goods evaluated at the new prices, then he consumes a different combination of goods, which determines a standard of living higher than that which he enjoyed in the first period."

Let I_{01}^0 be the true cost of living index computed on the standard determined by investigation of consumers in the base period, and let I_{01}^1 be the true index computed on the standard determined by investigation of consumers in the period of computation. The limits of I_{01}^0 and I_{01}^1 are then determined by Konüs as follows:

(a) $I_{01}^0 < L$ (Laspeyres' index)

(b) $I_{01}^1 > P$ (Paasche's index)

Result (a) is a direct consequence of the above theorem applied to situation 0, a diagramatic representation of which is shown in Fig. 4.3a. Passing through q_0 on the indifference surface A_0, the budget plane in situation 1 is tangent at q_1 to the indifference surface A_1, which is on the right-hand side of A_0 and therefore stands for higher utility than A_0. Thus, q_1 represents a higher standard than q_0. The same theorem applied to situation 1 leads to result (b), a diagramatic representation of which is shown in Fig. 4.3b. Passing through q_1' on A_1', the budget plane in situation 0 is tangent at q_0' to

A_0', which is on the right-hand side of A_1' and therefore stands for a higher utility than A_1'. Thus, q_0' represents a higher standard than q_1'.

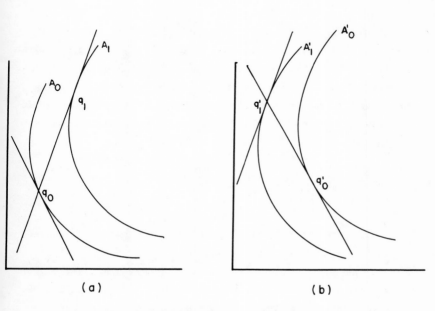

FIG. 4.3. A Diagramtic Representation of the First Theorem of Konüs.

Since I_{01}^0 may be either greater or smaller than I_{01}^1, neither of them need necessarily lie between L and P. If, on the other hand, I_{01}^0 were equal to I_{01}^1, it follows from the above that the true index would lie between L and P.

The next theorem proved is that "between the standard of living of consumers of the base period and the standard of living of consumers of the given period there always exists some standard for which the true index of the cost of living falls between Laspeyres' index and Paasche's index." If the true index for this intermediate standard is denoted by I_{01}^{ϵ}, then the theorem states that

$$L \gtrless I_{01}^{\epsilon} \gtrless P$$

Konüs then sets himself the task of finding a necessary condition for ensuring an approximate equality of the standards of living of the base period and the period compared. When this condition is satisfied, the true index of the cost of living is the ratio of the two expenditures in the two periods and would lie between L and P. Konüs proves that the two standards of living are equal if

$$\frac{\Sigma\, p_1 q_1}{\Sigma\, p_0 q_0} = \frac{\Sigma\, p_1 q_0}{\Sigma\, p_0 q_1}$$

Konüs further shows that neither of the budgetary indexes (i.e., L or P) can define the true change in the cost of living. He then indicates a method of determining the weights to be used in computing the true index. The method indicates, in effect, what "quantities should be consumed to guarantee a constant standard of living despite a given change in prices."

4.9. APPROACH MADE BY A. WALD

A. Wald [64] has made a significant contribution to the econometric aspects of the problem of computing the true index. The following is Wald's explanation of how he approached the problem:

Let us consider two time periods 0 and 1, denote by p_0^1, ..., p_0^n, the prices in the period 0, and by p_1^1, ..., p_1^n, the prices in the period 1. We suppose that we know the Engel curves C_0 and C_1 in the time periods 0 and 1. We have to calculate for each income* E_0 of the period 0 the equivalent income E_1 in the period 1. We say that the income E_1 in the period 1 is equivalent to the income E_0 in the period 0, if E_1 is the smallest income which enables us to buy with the prices of the period 1 a set of goods lying on the same indifference surface as the set of goods bought by E_0 in the period 0. The ratio E_1/E_0 between equivalent incomes is called the index of cost of living of the period 1 relative to the period 0 as basis.

Let us denote this index by $P_{01}(E_0)$. The index depends in general on the income E_0.

We shall next indicate the derivation of the formula. Let us denote by $q_0 = q_0^1,\ q_0^2,\ \ldots,\ q_0^n$ a point on the Engle curve C_0 and determine two points q_1 and $\hat{q}_1$ on the Engel curve C_1 such that

$$\Sigma\, p_0(q_1 - q_0) = \Sigma\, p_1(\hat{q}_1 - q_0) = 0 \qquad (4.11)$$

where the summation is over all goods. Such points q_1 and $\hat{q}_1$ certainly exist. If it should happen that q_1 is equal to $\hat{q}_1$, then by (4.11)

$$\Sigma\, p_0 q_1 = \Sigma\, p_0 q_0 \quad \text{and} \quad \Sigma\, p_1 q_1 = \Sigma\, p_1 q_0$$

From the first of these equations follows $I(q_0) \geq I(q_1)$ and from the second follows $I(q_0) \leq I(q_1)$, where $I(q)$ denotes an indicator, since at the price situation p_0 the utility is maximized at q_0, and at the price situation p_1 the utility is maximized at q_1. Hence, $I(q_0) = I(q_1)$ and $P_{01}(E_0) = \Sigma\, p_1 q_1 / \Sigma\, p_0 q_0$. The problem of constructing an index number can

---

*By "income" is understood the total expenditure for consumer goods.

then be solved exactly, using only the empirical data p_0, p_1, q_0, q_1.

Let us consider the case $q_1 \neq \hat{q}_1$. The points q_1 and $\hat{q}_1$ are near the point q_0 if the two Engel curves C_0 and C_1 are not very far from each other. Curves C_0 and C_1 can be distant from each other only if the price ratios in the period 0 are very different from the price ratios in the period 1. This, in general, is not the case if the time periods compared are not too distant.

Let us denote by $\hat{q}_0$ an arbitrary point on C_0 in the neighborhood of q_0 such that

$$\Sigma \, p_1(\hat{q}_0 - q_0) \neq 0$$

In order to determine an approximation to the index of the cost of living, we shall make the following assumption:

The indicator $I(q)$ can be approximated by a polynomial of the second degree in q $(= q', \ldots, q^n)$ in the tetrahedron T determined by the four points q_0, $\hat{q}_0$, q_1, $\hat{q}_1$.

If the tetrahedron T is small, the assumption is justified

If r_0 is a point on C_0 and r_1 is a point on C_1, both lying in the tetrahedron T, then because of the assumption the following equation can easily be deduced:

$$I(r_1) - I(r_0) = \frac{1}{2} \sum_{i=1}^{n} \left[\frac{\delta I(r_0)}{\delta q^i} + \frac{\delta I(r_1)}{\delta q^i} \right] (r_1^i - r_0^i)$$

$$= \frac{1}{2} \Sigma \, (\omega_0 p_0 + \omega_1 p_1)(r_1 - r_0) \qquad (4.12)$$

where ω_t denotes the marginal utility of money in r_t ($t = 0, 1$), that is, the value of the common ratio in the optimum conditions referred to in (4.5).

If $\bar{\gamma}_0$ and $\bar{\bar{\gamma}}_0$ are two points on C_0 and $\bar{\gamma}_1$ and $\bar{\bar{\gamma}}_1$ are two points on C_1, all lying in the tetrahedron T, we similarly get

$$I(\bar{\bar{\gamma}}_t) - I(\bar{\gamma}_t) = \frac{\bar{\omega}_t + \bar{\bar{\omega}}_t}{2} \sum p_t(\bar{\bar{\gamma}}_t - \bar{\gamma}_t), \quad t = 0, 1 \qquad (4.13)$$

From (4.12) and (4.13), we derive

$$\sum (\omega_1 p_1 + \omega_0 p_0)(q_0 - q_1) + (\omega_0 + \hat{\omega}_0) \sum p_0(\hat{q}_0 - q_0)$$

$$+ \sum (\omega_1 p_1 + \hat{\omega}_0 p_0)(q_1 - \hat{q}_0)$$

$$= 2\{[I(q_0) - I(q_1)] + [I(\hat{q}_0) - I(q_0)] + [I(q_1) - I(\hat{q}_0)]\}$$

$$= 0 \qquad (4.14)$$

and

$$\sum (\omega_0 p_0 + \omega_1 p_1)(q_1 - q_0) + (\omega_1 + \hat{\omega}_1) \sum p_1(\hat{q}_1 - q_1)$$

$$+ \sum (\omega_0 p_0 + \hat{\omega}_1 p_1)(q_0 - \hat{q}_1)$$

$$= 2\{[I(q_1) - I(q_0)] + [I(\hat{q}_1) - I(q_1)] + [I(q_0) - I(\hat{q}_1)]\}$$

$$= 0 \qquad (4.15)$$

where ω_t and $\hat{\omega}_t$ denote the marginal utility of money in q_t and $\hat{q}_t$ ($t = 0, 1$), respectively.

From (4.11) and (4.14) we get

$$\frac{\omega_1}{\omega_0} = \frac{\sum p_0(\hat{q}_0 - q_0)}{\sum p_1(\hat{q}_0 - q_0)} = \lambda \quad (\text{say})$$

and from (4.11) and (4.15) we get

$$\frac{\hat{\omega}_1}{\omega_0} = \frac{\sum p_0(\hat{q}_1 - q_1)}{\sum p_1(\hat{q}_1 - q_1)} = \mu \quad (\text{say}) \tag{4.17}$$

Since $I(q)$ is continuous,[*] there exists a point $\bar{q}_1$ on C_1 such that

$$I(\bar{q}_1) = I(q_0) \tag{4.18}$$

Our aim is to find the point $\bar{q}_1$. On the basis of Wald's assumption of linearity of the Engel curves, the point $\bar{q}_1$ can be taken to lie on the line $q_1\hat{q}_1$. Let the coordinates of the point $\bar{q}_1$ be given by $(\hat{q}_1 + xq_1)/(1 + x)$, where x is a constant to be determined. From (4.12) and (4.18) , we have

$$\frac{1}{2} \sum (\bar{\omega}_1 p_1 + \omega_0 p_0)(\bar{q}_1 - q_0)$$

$$= \frac{1}{2} \sum (\bar{\omega}_1 p_1 + \omega_0 p_0) \left(\frac{\hat{q}_1 + xq_1}{1 + x} - q_0 \right)$$

$$= I(\bar{q}_1) - I(q_0) = 0$$

Hence, with the help of (4.11) ,

$$x = \frac{\omega_0}{\bar{\omega}_1} \frac{\sum p_0(\hat{q}_1 - q_1)}{\sum p_1(\hat{q}_1 - q_1)}$$

$$= \frac{\omega_0}{\bar{\omega}_1} \frac{\hat{\omega}_1}{\omega_0} = \frac{\hat{\omega}_1}{\bar{\omega}_1} \tag{4.19}$$

the second equality following from (4.17) . Again, with the help of (4.12) , (4.13) , and (4.18) , we have

---

[*]This simplified derivation is taken from K.S. Banerjee [10].

$$[I(q_1) - I(q_0)] + [I(\bar{q}_1) - I(q_1)]$$

$$= \frac{1}{2} \sum (\omega_0 p_0 + \omega_1 p_1)(q_1 - q_0) + \frac{\omega_1 + \bar{\omega}_1}{2} \sum p_1\left(\frac{\hat{q}_1 + xq_1}{1 + x} - q_1\right)$$

$$= 0$$

Hence,

$$x = \bar{\omega}_1/\omega_1 \tag{4.20}$$

Multiplying (4.19) and (4.20), we get

$$x^2 = \frac{\bar{\omega}_1}{\omega_1} \frac{\hat{\omega}_1}{\bar{\omega}_1} = \frac{\hat{\omega}_1}{\omega_1} = \frac{\mu}{\lambda}$$

or

$$x = \sqrt{\mu/\lambda}$$

The positive value of x is admitted since the ratios of the marginal utilities are nonnegative. Therefore, $\bar{q}_1$ is determined. We have, finally,

$$P_{01}(E_0) = \frac{E_1}{E_0} = \frac{\sum p_1 \bar{q}_1}{\sum p_0 q_0} = \frac{\sum p_1(\hat{q}_1 + q_1 \sqrt{\mu/\lambda})}{\sum p_0 q_0(1 + \sqrt{\mu/\lambda})}$$

$$\equiv \frac{\sum p_1(q_0 + q_1 \sqrt{\mu/\lambda})}{\sum p_0(q_0 + q_1 \sqrt{\mu/\lambda})} \tag{4.21}$$

The last equality follows from Eq. (4.11).

Wald eventually showed that this index lies between the limits of L_p and P_p, where L_p and P_p denote, respectively, Laspeyres' and Paasche's aggregative price indexes.

A Remark. The above shows that, corresponding to the point $\bar{q}_1$ on the segment $q_1\hat{q}_1$, there exists a point q^* on the line q_0q_1 such that

$$I(q_0) = I(\bar{q}_1) = I(q^*) \tag{4.22}$$

The point q^* divides the intercept $q_0 q_1$ in the same ratio $x:1$ as the point $\bar{q}_1$ divides the segment $\hat{q}_1 q_1$. The line $q^* \bar{q}_1$ is parallel to $q_0 \hat{q}_1$. There is therefore an Engel curve C^* between C_0 and C_1 that passes through the budget plane connecting q_1 and q_0 at q^* which satisfies (4.21).

The points $\bar{q}_1$ and q^* are indicated in Fig. 4.4, which has been drawn in the same manner as given in Wald.

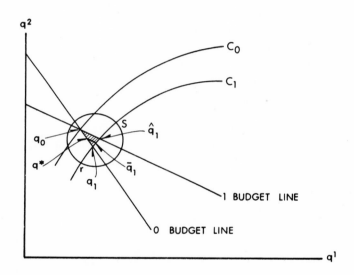

FIG. 4.4. Engel curves and the budget lines.

Reduction of the Formula to a Practicable Form. Wald then reduced the formula in terms of the estimates of the parameters of the Engel curves.

Suppose the Engel curves C_0 and C_1 are given by the following equations:

The equations of C_0: $\quad q_0^i = \alpha_0^i E + \beta_0^i$

The equations of C_1: $\quad q_1^i = \alpha_1^i E + \beta_1^i$

$\left.\right\}$ $i = 1, 2, \ldots, n$

We introduce the notations $\Sigma \alpha_j^i p_k^i = a_{jk}$ and $\Sigma \beta_j^i p_k^i = b_{jk}$ (j, k = 0, 1), where the summation is over all goods. It is obvious that $a_{11} = a_{00} = 1$, and $b_{11} = b_{00} = 0$. We get from (4.16) and (4.17)

$$\lambda = \frac{a_{00}}{a_{01}} = \frac{1}{a_{01}} \quad \text{and} \quad \mu = \frac{a_{10}}{a_{11}} = a_{10} \tag{4.23}$$

From (4.11), we have

$$\Sigma \, p_0 q_0 = \Sigma \, p_0 q_1 = E_0 \tag{4.24}$$

Since $\Sigma \, p_1 q_1$ is equal to E_1 and therefore

$$q_1' = \alpha_1' E_1 + \beta_1', \ldots, q_1^n = \alpha_1^n E_1 + \beta_1^n$$

we get, from (4.11),

$$a_{10} E_1 + b_{10} = E_0$$

Hence,

$$E_1 = \frac{E_0 - b_{10}}{a_{10}} = \Sigma \, p_1 q_1 \tag{4.25}$$

It is obvious that

$$\Sigma \, p_1 q_0 = a_{01} E_0 + b_{01} \tag{4.26}$$

If we substitute in (4.21) for λ, μ, $\Sigma \, p_1 q_0$, $\Sigma \, p_1 q_1$, $\Sigma \, p_0 q_0$, and $\Sigma \, p_0 q_1$ their expressions from (4.23) through (4.26),

$$P_{01}(E_0) = \frac{a_{01} + \sqrt{a_{10} a_{01}}/a_{10}}{1 + \sqrt{a_{01} a_{10}}} + \frac{1}{E_0} \frac{b_{01} - b_{10}\sqrt{a_{01} a_{10}}/a_{10}}{1 + \sqrt{a_{01} a_{10}}}$$

$$\tag{4.27}$$

or

$$P_{01}(E_0) = \sqrt{\frac{a_{01}}{a_{10}}} + \frac{1}{E_0} \frac{b_{01} - b_{10}\sqrt{a_{01}a_{10}}/a_{10}}{1 + \sqrt{a_{01}a_{10}}} \qquad (4.28)$$

This is the formula sought. If the α and β coefficients for the Engel curves are statistically determined, all the magnitudes in (4.28) are known.

4.10. THE DOUBLE-EXPENDITURE METHOD OF RAGNAR FRISCH[*]

Let us denote by q_0 a point on the Engel curve C_0 and by q_1 a point on the Engel curve C_1. If the indicator $I(q)$ can be approximated by a polynomial of the second degree, then

$$I(q_1) - I(q_0) = \frac{1}{2} \Sigma (\omega_0 p_0 + \omega_1 p_1)(q_1 - q_0)$$

$$= \frac{1}{2} (\omega_0 \Sigma p_0 q_1 - \omega_1 \Sigma p_1 q_0)$$

$$+ \frac{1}{2} (\omega_1 \Sigma p_1 q_1 - \omega_0 \Sigma p_0 q_0)$$

where ω_t ($t = 0, 1$) denotes the marginal utility of money in the point q_t. Hence, for a point q_1, for which $I(q_1) = I(q_0)$, the following equation holds:

$$(\omega_0 \Sigma p_0 q_1 - \omega_1 \Sigma p_1 q_0) + (\omega_1 \Sigma p_1 q_1 - \omega_0 \Sigma p_0 q_0) = 0$$

$$(4.29)$$

Frisch makes the assumption that, if $I(q_1) = I(q_0)$, then the relation

$$\frac{\omega_1}{\omega_0} = \frac{\Sigma p_0 q_0}{\Sigma p_1 q_1} \qquad (4.30)$$

---

[*]This exposition is taken from Wald [64].

is valid approximately. From (4.29) and (4.30) it follows that, if $I(q_1) = I(q_0)$, then

$$\Sigma\, p_1 q_1 \, \Sigma\, p_0 q_1 = \Sigma\, p_1 q_0 \, \Sigma\, p_0 q_0$$

If a point q_0 on C_0 is given, we determine the point q_1 on C_1 for which $I(q_1) = I(q_0)$ by choosing that point q_1 on C_1 for which the following equation holds:

$$\Sigma\, p_1 q_1 \, \Sigma\, p_0 q_1 = \Sigma\, p_1 q_0 \, \Sigma\, p_0 q_0$$

The left-hand side of the above equation is the product of expenditures on q_1 at prices p_1 and p_0 (double expenditure), while the right-hand side is the product of expenditures on q_0 at the prices p_1 and p_0 (double expenditure).

Finally, we want to calculate the index formula of the double-expenditure method under the assumption that the Engel curves C_0 and C_1 are linear. With the same notation as in Sec. 4.9, we have

$$\Sigma\, p_0 q_0 = E_0, \ \Sigma\, p_0 q_1 = \Sigma\, \alpha_1 p_0 E_1 + \Sigma\, \beta_1 p_0 = a_{10} E_1 + b_{10}$$

$$\Sigma\, p_1 q_0 = \Sigma\, \alpha_0 p_1 E_0 + \Sigma\, \beta_0 p_1 = a_{01} E_0 + b_{01}, \ \Sigma\, p_1 q_1 = E_1$$

According to the double-expenditure method, the point q_1, which is equivalent to q_0, is given by the equation

$$\Sigma\, p_0 q_0 \, \Sigma\, p_1 q_0 = \Sigma\, p_0 q_1 \, \Sigma\, p_1 q_1$$

If we substitute for $\Sigma\, p_0 q_0$, $\Sigma\, p_0 q_1$, $\Sigma\, p_1 q_0$, $\Sigma\, p_1 q_1$ in the above expressions, we get

$$E_0(a_{01} E_0 + b_{01}) = E_1(a_{10} E_1 + b_{10})$$

Hence,

$$E_1 = \frac{-b_{10} + \sqrt{b_{10}^2 + 4a_{10}a_{01}E_0^2 + 4a_{10}b_{01}E_0}}{2a_{10}}$$

and

$$P_{01}(E_0) = \frac{-b_{10} + \sqrt{b_{10}^2 + 4a_{10}a_{01}E_0^2 + 4a_{10}b_{01}E_0}}{2a_{10}E_0} \qquad (4.31)$$

This index formula is equivalent to formula (4.28) if

$$(a_{10}b_{01})^2 = a_{10}a_{01}(b_{10})^2$$

4.11.   FACTORIAL APPROACH TO THE CONSTRUCTION OF THE TRUE INDEX OF COST OF LIVING

Preliminary Remarks. Since the factorial approach to the construction of the true index is of recent origin and since, perhaps, the approach is relatively less known that others, let us start by recalling the definition of true index.

The problem of constructing the true index of cost of living can be described as that of determining money incomes (expenditures) that yield equivalent satisfaction, or the same standard of living (i.e., the same general status of want satisfaction), in two or more periods of time characterized by different price situations. The ratio of such expenditures in two different periods of time gives the true index of cost of living of one period with reference to the other.

To the best of this author's knowledge, Wald [64] was the first to present an exact solution (in the mathematical sense) of the problem under a suitable mathematical formulation. Wald's formula, as we have seen, is dependent on several simplifying assumptions. His index lies between the same limits of L_p and P_p as the index of Konüs. However, even if a solution were

exact in the mathematical sense, its reduction to a usable form
would eventually have to appeal to statistical considerations.
For example, Wald's formula was finally presented in terms of
the estimated parameters of Engel's curves.

Origin of the Factorial Approach and What It Provides.
G. Stuvel [59] gave new formulas for price and quantity indexes
which emerged from a study of "value change" in international
trade, resulting from change in price and quantity (volume).
Stuvel's formulation of the problem with reference to the price
and quantity compoents is analogous to that usually adopted to
describe factorial effects in the design of experiments. This
phenomenon made it possible to give an orientation to Stuvel's
approach in the perspective of the design of experiments and,
with this orientation, it was possible to work out several gen-
eralizations and extensions. The extensions provided, among
other things, multidimensional indexes [14,17,18,20] and indexes
(Appendix E) that are comparable to the best linear index numbers given by H. Theil. In the setup of factorial experiments,
it was easy to recognize that value change could be thought of
as the sum of two orthogonal components (independent), one due
to price and the other due to quantity. This property could be
exploited [17] to split the index of national income or value
index in any other form into the components of the price index
and the quantity index. The factorial approach also provided a
new interpretation of Laspeyres' and Paasche's indexes, as we
shall see later in this section. In fact, it appeared that the
entire problem of constructing price and quantity indexes could
perhaps be studied under the unified treatment of the factorial
approach.

Conversely, it was visualized [19] that index number formulas might also be used in the interpretation of results in
the design of experiments.

The aim of this section is to provide an outline of the
factorial approach that was adopted in constructing the true
index of cost of living. Most of this section is a review, except where it is demonstrated that, like the formulas of Konüs
and Wald, the true index, constructed on the factorial approach,
also lies between L_p and P_p. (That the true index lies between these limits was mentioned by the author in ref. [18],
although the details of derivation were not presented.)

   Stuvel's Formulas. Before the basic steps of the factorial
approach are described, it is necessary to refer briefly to the
derivation of Stuvel's formulas. In working out a method for
obtaining unbiased measures of the effect of changes in the
terms of trade on a country's foreign balance on current account,
Stuvel proceeded in the following manner:

   The value V of the transactions in any given commodity i
during any given period, whether it be the base year 0 or the
current year 1, is equal to the product of quantity q and
price p. Consequently, the value of the transactions in this
commodity in the current year V_1^i can be related to the value
of the transactions in this commodity in the base year V_0^i
through multiplication of the latter value with the appropriate
volume and price relatives κ_1^i, π_1^i, which are equal to q_1^i/q_0^i
and p_1^i/p_0^i, respectively. Thus,

$$V_1 = V_0^i \kappa_1^i \pi_1^i \quad \text{for} \quad V_1^i/V_0^i = q_1^i p_1^i / q_0^i p_0^i$$

   For an additive analysis of value changes, two different
formulas suggest themselves; one has the choice of using the
base year volume valued at the current year price, $q_0^i p_1^i = V_0^i \pi_1^i$,
or the current year volume valued at the base year price,
$q_1^i p_0^i = V_1^i/\pi_1^i = V_0^i \kappa^i$, as a means of separating the volume effect
from the price effect. The formulas concerned are

$$V_1^i - V_0^i = (V_1^i - V_0^i \pi^i) + (V_0^i \pi^i - V_0^i)$$

$$= V_0^i \pi^i (\kappa^i - 1) + V_0^i (\pi^i - 1) \tag{4.32a}$$

$$V_1^i - V_0^i = (V_1^i - V_0^i \kappa^i) + (V_0^i \kappa^i - V_0^i)$$

$$= V_0^i \kappa^i (\pi^i - 1) + V_0^i (\kappa^i - 1) \tag{4.32b}$$

Stuvel [59] then took an average of the above two identities to represent value change for the ith commodity in the following form:

$$V_1^i - V_0^i = V_0^i (\pi^i \kappa^i - 1)$$

$$= \frac{V_0^i}{2} (\pi^i + 1)(\kappa^i - 1) + \frac{V_0^i}{2} (\pi^i - 1)(\kappa^i + 1) \tag{4.33}$$

where $V_1^i = p_1^i q_1^i$; $V_0^i = p_0^i q_0^i$; $\pi^i = p_1^i / p_0^i$; $\kappa^i = q_1^i / q_0^i$; p_1^i and q_1^i are, respectively, the price and the quantity in the period 1 (the period of comparison); p_0^i and q_0^i are, respectively, the price and the quantity in the period 0 (the base period); and π^i and κ^i are, respectively, the price and quantity indexes for the ith commodity $(i = 1, 2, \ldots, r)$.

Summing up Eq. (4.33) over r commodities, we get

$$\sum_i V_1^i - \sum_i V_0^i = \sum_i \frac{V_0^i (\pi^i + 1)(\kappa^i - 1)}{2} + \sum_i \frac{V_0^i (\pi^i - 1)(\kappa^i + 1)}{2}$$

$$= \sum_i A^i + \sum_i B^i \tag{4.34}$$

where $A^i \equiv \frac{1}{2} V_0^i (\pi^i + 1)(\kappa^i - 1)$, and $B^i \equiv \frac{1}{2} V_0^i (\pi^i - 1)(\kappa^i + 1)$.

Equation (4.34) can be written as $V_1 - V_0 = A + B$, where $V_1 \equiv \Sigma_i V_1^i$, $V_0 \equiv \Sigma_i V_0^i$, $A \equiv \Sigma_i A_1^i$, and $B \equiv \Sigma_i B_1^i$.

The conditions that index numbers must satisfy are

$$\frac{V_0(\pi + 1)(\kappa - 1)}{2} = \sum_i \frac{V_0^i(\pi^i + 1)(\kappa^i - 1)}{2}$$

$$(4.35)$$

$$\frac{V_0(\pi - 1)(\kappa + 1)}{2} = \sum_i \frac{V_0^i(\pi^i - 1)(\kappa^i + 1)}{2}$$

where π and κ are the required price and quantity indexes. Solutions of Eqs. (4.35) lead to the price and quantity indexes as follows:

$$\pi = \frac{L_p - L_q}{2} + \sqrt{\left(\frac{L_p - L_q}{2}\right)^2 + \frac{V_1}{V_0}} \qquad (4.36a)$$

$$\kappa = \frac{L_q - L_p}{2} + \sqrt{\left(\frac{L_q - L_p}{2}\right)^2 + \frac{V_1}{V_0}} \qquad (4.36b)$$

where L_p and L_q denote, respectively, Laspeyres' (or base-weighted) indexes of price and quantity (volume), and V_1 and V_0, as stated before, are the values of the aggregate in the current period 1 and the base period 0, respectively.

These formulas have many desirable properties [59]. For example, they meet the factor reversal and the time reversal tests, which, as we know, are not satisfied by Laspeyres' and Paasche's formulas.

A Basic Assumption in the Factorial Approach. In an in-genious interpretation of index numbers by Divisia and Roy (see Appendix A), it was assumed that the sum Σ pq could be denoted by the product P^*Q^*, where P^* represents a general price level and Q^* denotes a measure of physical volume of goods. In a similar manner, we could also assume the following:

$$\Sigma \; p_0 q_0 = P_0^* Q_0^* \quad \Sigma \; p_0 q_1 = P_0^* Q_1^*$$
$$\Sigma \; p_1 q_0 = P_1^* Q_0^* \quad \Sigma \; p_1 q_1 = P_1^* Q_1^* \tag{4.37}$$

The above relations hold for single commodities. We require that these relationships hold for an aggregate over r commodities. Such an assumption is also inherent in Eqs. (4.35) of Stuvel.

<u>Description of a 2^2-Fractorial Experiment</u>. The analytical procedure of a "2^2-factorial" in the design of experiments is well known. A 2^2-factorial is an experiment with two factors at two levels each. Let the factors be price p and quantity q, and let the levels be 0 and 1, giving the four factorial combinations as $p_0 q_0$, $p_1 q_0$, $p_0 q_1$, and $p_1 q_1$. These four combinations are abbreviated as 1, p, q, and pq, the presence of a letter denoting the presence of the corresponding factor. If, as usual, the capital letters stand for the factorial effects and the small letters represent the factors, the main effects P and Q and the interaction PQ from one replication are given by

$$P = \frac{1}{2} \left(-p_0 q_0 + p_1 q_0 - p_0 q_1 + p_1 q_1 \right) \equiv \frac{1}{2} (p - 1)(q + 1)$$

$$Q = \frac{1}{2} \left(-p_0 q_0 - p_1 q_0 + p_0 q_1 + p_1 q_1 \right) \equiv \frac{1}{2} (p + 1)(q - 1)$$

$$PQ = \frac{1}{2} \left(p_0 q_0 - p_1 q_0 - p_0 q_1 + p_1 q_1 \right) \equiv \frac{1}{2} (p - 1)(q - 1) \tag{4.38}$$

The above main effects and the interaction can be conveniently represented in schematic form:

Effect   1 p q pq

$$
\begin{array}{l}
\text{Mean} \\
\text{P} \\
\text{Q} \\
\text{PQ}
\end{array}
=
\begin{bmatrix}
+ & + & + & + \\
- & + & - & + \\
- & - & + & + \\
+ & - & - & +
\end{bmatrix}
\qquad (4.39)
$$

where "mean" stands for a general effect. The above scheme
shows with what sign a factorial combination of the two factors
will appear in a main effect or the interaction. Conversely,
it also shows with what sign a main effect or the interaction
will enter into the expression denoting a factorial combination.
For example,

$$P = \frac{1}{2} (-1 + p - q + pq)$$

$$PQ = \frac{1}{2} (1 - p - q + pq)$$

$$pq = \text{mean} + \frac{1}{2} (P + Q + PQ)$$

$$pq - 1 = P + Q \quad \text{etc.}$$

The above scheme of signs represents a 4×4 orthogonal
matrix (Hadamard matrix), where "+" is interpreted as +1 and
"-" is interpreted as -1.

If there are r replications, Eqs. (4.38) have the same
forms, where an average $\Sigma\, p_j q_k / r$ is substituted for $p_j q_k$
(j, k = 0, 1). For example, the main effect P is given by

$$P = \frac{1}{2r} (- \Sigma\, p_0 q_0 + \Sigma\, p_1 q_0 - \Sigma\, p_0 q_1 + \Sigma\, p_1 q_1)$$

The Factorial Approach. As the scheme of signs in (4.39)
indicates, four mutually orthogonal linear combinations can be
formed of the four totals, $\Sigma\, p_j q_k$ (j, k = 0, 1). Writing
$\Sigma\, p_j q_k = P_j^* Q_k^*$, in consonance with Eqs. (4.37), we have

$$P_0^*Q_0^* + P_1^*Q_0^* + P_0^*Q_1^* + P_1^*Q_1^* \equiv (P_1^* + P_0^*)(Q_1^* + Q_0^*) \quad (4.40a)$$

$$-P_0^*Q_0^* + P_1^*Q_0^* - P_0^*Q_1^* + P_1^*Q_1^* \equiv (P_1^* - P_0^*)(Q_1^* + Q_0^*) \quad (4.40b)$$

$$-P_0^*Q_0^* - P_1^*Q_0^* + P_0^*Q_1^* + P_1^*Q_1^* \equiv (P_1^* + P_0^*)(Q_1^* - Q_0^*) \quad (4.40c)$$

$$+P_0^*Q_0^* - P_1^*Q_0^* - P_0^*Q_1^* + P_1^*Q_1^* \equiv (P_1^* - P_0^*)(Q_1^* - Q_0^*) \quad (4.40d)$$

In Eqs. (4.40) an asterisk distinguishes a capital letter from the corresponding main effect.

Let

$$+ \Sigma \, p_0 q_0 + \Sigma \, p_1 q_0 + \Sigma \, p_0 q_1 + \Sigma \, p_1 q_1 \equiv a$$

$$- \Sigma \, p_0 q_0 + \Sigma \, p_1 q_0 - \Sigma \, p_0 q_1 + \Sigma \, p_1 q_1 \equiv b$$

$$- \Sigma \, p_0 q_0 - \Sigma \, p_1 q_0 + \Sigma \, p_0 q_1 + \Sigma \, p_1 q_1 \equiv c \qquad (4.41)$$

$$+ \Sigma \, p_0 q_0 - \Sigma \, p_1 q_0 - \Sigma \, p_0 q_1 + \Sigma \, p_1 q_1 \equiv d$$

Hence, for identities (4.40) and (4.41) we have the following equations:

$$\frac{V_0(\pi + 1)(\kappa + 1)}{2} = \frac{a}{2} \qquad (4.42a)$$

$$\frac{V_0(\pi - 1)(\kappa + 1)}{2} = \frac{b}{2} \qquad (4.42b)$$

$$\frac{V_0(\pi + 1)(\kappa - 1)}{2} = \frac{c}{2} \qquad (4.42c)$$

$$\frac{V_0(\pi - 1)(\kappa - 1)}{2} = \frac{d}{2} \qquad (4.42d)$$

where $P_1^*/P_0^* = \pi$ (required price index), $Q_1^*/Q_0^* = \kappa$ (required quantity index), and $\Sigma \, p_0 q_0 = P_0^*Q_0^* = V_0$. (Recall that, in the terminology of the design of experiments, $b/2r$, $c/2r$, and $d/2r$ denote, respectively, the main effects P and Q and the interaction PQ.)

From the four identities in (4.42), six pairs of equations in π and κ can be formed, and the equations can be solved for π and κ. But all six pairs of equations are not equally meaningful. Of these pairs, the pair with (4.42b) and (4.42c) is the following:

$$V_0(\pi - 1)(\kappa + 1) = 2rP = a \qquad (4.43a)$$

$$V_0(\pi + 1)(\kappa - 1) = 2rQ = b \qquad (4.43b)$$

The above equations are the same as those obtained by Stuvel. Solutions for π and κ are given in (4.36a) and (4.36b), respectively. Notice that these two equations take into account the effect of price and quantity in value change.

Solutions from Eqs. (4.42b) and (4.42d), which recognize the effect of price and the interaction[*] between price and quantity in value change give the price and quantity indexes as follows:

$$\pi(\text{price index}) = L_p \qquad (4.44a)$$

$$\kappa(\text{quantity index}) = \frac{V_1/V_0 - L_q}{L_p - 1} \qquad (4.44b)$$

Such a pair cannot represent the true state of value change, because it takes into account the effect of price and the interaction between price and quantity in value change, but not the effects of price and quantity. Similarly, Eqs. (4.42c)

---

[*] If, in value change, threre were no joint effect of quantity and price change, the first component of (4.32b) and the second component of (4.32a) would be identical. Their difference, if any, can therefore be interpreted as the "interaction" between price change and quantity change. Similarly, in the absence of a joint effect of price and quantity change, the difference between the first component of (4.32a) and the second component of (4.32b) would be the same "interaction" between price and quantity change.

and $(4.42d)$ take into account the effect of quantity and the
interaction between price and quantity in value change, but not
the effects of price and quantity, lead to the following solutions:

$$\pi(\text{price index}) = \frac{V_1/V_0 - L_p}{L_q - 1} \qquad (4.45a)$$

$$\kappa(\text{quantity index}) = L_q \qquad\qquad (4.45b)$$

Other pairs are less meaningful. For example, the pair
$(4.42a)$ and $(4.42b)$ takes into account the effect of the "mean"
(i.e., a general effect) and the interaction between price and
quantity in value change. Such a situation is very unrealistic.
The indexes in (4.44) and (4.45) do not satisfy the time reversal and the factor reversal tests, while the indexes obtained
from the pair $(4.42b)$ and $(4.42c)$ do.

This approach to deriving the indexes, as observed above,
lends a new interpretation to Laspeyres' price and quantity indexes as given in (4.44) and (4.45). In one instance, $(4.44b)$
is the mate of Laspeyres' price index L_p and, in the other,
$(4.45a)$ is the mate of Laspeyres' quantity index L_q.

Formulation of the True Index. Let a quantity q_1 be found
in situation 1 (period of comparison) such that the quantity
index κ_{01} of the quantity q_1 compared to q_0 is unity.
Then, q_1 is regarded as equivalent to q_0 from the point of
view of the standard of living. The price index π_{01}, based on
such a formulation, should therefore represent the true index
of cost of living. In support of this formulation, we make the
following observations. Fisher's ideal formulas for price and
quantity are given by

$$F_p = \sqrt{\frac{V_{10}V_{11}}{V_{00}V_{01}}}$$

$$F_q = \sqrt{\frac{V_{01}V_{11}}{V_{00}V_{10}}}$$

where $V_{jk} = \Sigma_i\, p_j^i q_k^i$ (j, k = 0, 1). (In terms of the notations used by Stuvel, $V_{11} = V_1$, and $V_{00} = V_0$.) If $F_q = 1$, the price index reduces to V_{11}/V_{00}. The condition $F_q = 1$ implies that $V_{11}V_{01} = V_{10}V_{00}$, that is,

$$\Sigma\, p_1 q_1\, \Sigma\, p_0 q_1 = \Sigma\, p_1 q_0\, \Sigma\, p_0 q_0 \qquad\qquad (4.46)$$

Condition (4.46) is known as the condition of double expenditure of Ragnar Frisch, which he used in deriving the true index. This is also the condition suggested by A. A. Konüs in deriving the approximate formula for the true index of cost of living. It may also be recalled that Wald's derivation of the formula for the true index depended on the following initial assumptions:

$$\Sigma p_0(q_1 - q_0) = 0 = \Sigma\, p_1(\hat{q}_1 - q_0) \qquad\qquad (4.47)$$

The first identity of (4.47) implies that L_q is equal to 1, and the second implies that P_q (Paasche) is equal to 1.

This condition of equivalence can now be applied to the quantity index (4.36b). Let the quantity index κ given by (4.36b) be equated to 1 to get the equivalent q_1. Substituting $\kappa = 1$ in Eq. (4.42c), we get

$$V_{11} - V_{10} + V_{01} - V_{00} = 0 \qquad\qquad (4.48)$$

Substituting condition (4.48) in (4.42b), which gives the corresponding price index, we get the true index of price (cost of living)

$$\pi = \frac{V_{11}}{V_{00}} \tag{4.49}$$

Notice that condition (4.48) is similar to condition (4.46), the condition worked out by Konüs and Frisch. Multiplication in (4.46) takes the place of addition in (4.48).

Limits of the True Index Obtained from the Factorial Approach. As stated before, the true index given by Konüs lies within the limits of Laspeyres' price index, L_p, and Paasche's price index, P_p. Wald's index also lies between the same limits. It is shown below that the true index, obtained from the factorial approach, also lies between L_p and P_p. From (4.48) we have

$$V_{11} - V_{00}L_p + \frac{V_{11}}{P_p} - V_{00} = 0$$

$$\geq \frac{V_{11}}{V_{00}} = \frac{P_p(L_p + 1)}{P_p + 1} \tag{4.50}$$

Following Konüs, let us make two possible hypotheses. First, let us suppose $V_{10} > V_{11}$. Then, from (4.48), $V_{01} > V_{00}$. This implies

$$\frac{V_{10}}{V_{00}} > \frac{V_{11}}{V_{01}}, \quad \text{i.e.,} \quad L_p > P_p$$

If $L_p > P_p$, from (4.50),

$$\frac{V_{11}}{V_{00}} > P_p$$

Again, since $V_{10} > V_{11}$,

$$\frac{V_{10}}{V_{00}} > \frac{V_{11}}{V_{00}}, \quad \text{i.e.,} \quad L_p > \frac{V_{11}}{V_{00}}$$

Thus,

$$L_p > \frac{V_{11}}{V_{00}} > P_p \qquad\qquad (4.51)$$

Let us now suppose the opposite, i.e., let $V_{10} < V_{11}$. Then, from (4.48), $V_{01} < V_{00}$. This implies

$$\frac{V_{10}}{V_{00}} < \frac{V_{11}}{V_{01}}, \quad \text{i.e.,} \quad L_p < P_p$$

If $L_p < P_p$, from (4.50),

$$\frac{V_{11}}{V_{00}} < P_p$$

Since $V_{10} < V_{11}$,

$$\frac{V_{10}}{V_{00}} < \frac{V_{11}}{V_{00}}, \quad \text{i.e.,} \quad L_p < \frac{V_{11}}{V_{00}}$$

Thus,

$$L_p < \frac{V_{11}}{V_{00}} < P_p \qquad\qquad (4.52)$$

Hence, combining (4.51) and (4.52), we have

$$L_p \gtrless \frac{V_{11}}{V_{00}} \gtrless P_p$$

The New Index Compared with Those of Wald and Frisch.
Index (4.49) can now be compared with those given by Wald and Frisch.

Suppose the Engel curves C_0 and C_1 are linear and are given by the following equations:

$$C_0: \quad q_0^i = \alpha_0^i v + \beta_0^i$$

$$C_1: \quad q_1^i = \alpha_1^i v + \beta_1^i$$

where v is the money income (expenditure). Let $\sum \alpha_j^i p_k^i = a_{jk}$ and $\sum \beta_j^i p_k^i = b_{jk}$ (j, k = 0, 1). Then, $a_{jj} = 1$ and $b_{jj} = 0$ (j = 0, 1). Also,

$$\sum p_0^i q_0^i = V_{00}, \quad \sum p_1^i q_1^i = V_{11}$$

$$\tag{4.53}$$

$$V_{01} = a_{10} V_{11} + b_{10}, \quad V_{10} = a_{01} V_{00} + b_{01}$$

In terms of the above coefficients, Frisch's true index, as evaluated by Wald, is given by

$$F = \frac{-b_{10} + \sqrt{b_{10}^2 + 4a_{10} a_{01} V_{00}^2 + 4a_{10} b_{01} V_{00}}}{2a_{10} V_{00}}$$

and Wald's true index is given by

$$W = \sqrt{\frac{a_{01}}{a_{10}}} + \frac{1}{V_{00}} \frac{b_{01} - b_{10} \sqrt{a_{01} a_{10}}/a_{10}}{1 + \sqrt{a_{01} a_{10}}}$$

The true index, from the factorial approach, is obtained by substituting the values of V_{01} and V_{10} from (4.53) in (4.48). The index finally reduces to

$$B = \frac{1 + a_{01}}{1 + a_{10}} + \frac{1}{V_{00}} \frac{b_{01} - b_{10}}{1 + a_{10}}$$

Wald pointed out that the index of Frisch reduces to the index of Wald if $(a_{10} b_{01})^2 = a_{10} a_{01} (b_{10})^2$. Again, when $a_{10} = a_{01}$, $W = B$. If, in addition, $b_{10} = b_{01}$, $F = W = B = 1$.

Chapter 5

SAMPLING IN THE CONSTRUCTION OF COST
OF LIVING INDEX (CONSUMER PRICE INDEX) NUMBERS

5.1. INTRODUCTION

In the computation of cost of living index numbers (consumer price index numbers), sampling is inevitable at several
points. A full account of the rationale for sampling has been
given by McCarthy [47], who makes mention of the different
stages that involve questions on sampling. The stages are as
follows:

1. Determination of the item weights (Consumer expendi-
    ture surveys or family budget inquiries).
2. Selection of the sample of cities for the index (in
    case the city indexes have to be combined to give a
    national index).
3. Selection of a sample of items of expenditure that
    is to be priced in computing the index.
4. Determination of the points in time at which price
    quotations for the "specified-in-detail" items (in-
    cluding constituent items of a composite commodity)
    are to be obtained.

5. Selection of a sample of price reporters from whom the
price quotations are obtained.

The discussion in this Chapter is devoted, however, only
to domain 3, and in this context we shall (a) introduce the
concept of an unbiased estimate for the index, indicate the
variance formula for the same and work out the principle of
optimum allocation [7]; (b) point out the implications of certain prevalent practices [9]; and (c) show how sampling errors
can be calculated for the estimated index under specified sampling procedures [15].

5.2. AN ASSUMPTION

It has been shown that Laspeyres' formula in the original
form (writing 1 and 0 above p and q) expressed as a percentage is

$$\frac{100 \sum p^1 q^0}{\sum p^0 q^0}$$

or, more explicitly,

$$\frac{100 \sum_i p_i^1 q_i^0}{\sum_i p_i^0 q_i^0} \tag{5.1}$$

where Σ extends over all items of consumption. When reduced,
it takes the following form

$$\frac{100 \sum_i (p_i^1/p_i^0) \, p_i^0 q_i^0}{\sum_i p_i^0 q_i^0} = \sum_i r_i w_i \tag{5.2}$$

where r_i is the price relative of the ith item expressed as
a percentage, and w_i is the proportion of expenditure of the
same ith item and is called its weight. The formula is expressed
in the form of a weighted average of price relatives, where the
sum of the weights equals unity.

The questionnaire adopted in a family budget inquiry (or
consumer expenditure survey) usually provides for items of expenditure that are either composite or single items. We shall
assume here that the items of consumption on which expenditure
is reported are, in all cases, composite commodities and that
each composite commodity consists of a group of single (speci-
fied-in-detail) items, finite in number. Moreover, we shall
make the simplifying assumption that composite commodities (commodity categories) are so chosen that for each composite commodity the expenditures on all constituent single items are the
same. In other words, this means that the component items within any commodity classification are of equal importance in consumption.

An illustration will make the implication of the assumption
clear. Vegetables occur as an item of consumption under food;
this item is composite. It should be possible to record the
expenditure incurred on vegetables as a whole, but it may be
impracticable to record expenditures separately on the constituent items of vegetables. Thus, to make the collection of information on expenditures practicable, provision is made in the
family budget inquiry questionnaire for recording expenditures
on composite commodities. Obviously, this compositeness cannot
be allowed to remain too broad. In order to have precision,
composite commodities are divided into subgroups. For example,
vegetables can be divided into such subgroups as leafy vegetables, potatoes, onions, and the rest of the nonleafy vegetables. Since each of these subgroups has an importance in consumption and is also composite, it should be possible to gather

information on the expenditure separately on such subgroups
when family budgets are collected.

It may not be necessary to carry the process of subdivision
down to single items. We shall assume, however, that the process of dividing a composite commodity into subgroups has been
carried down to a stage where it is reasonable to accept that
the constituent items of a subgroup have equal expenditures,
i.e., equal importance in consumption. For example, when the
subgroup leafy vegetables is provided for as an item in the
family budget inquiry schedule (questionnaire), it is assumed
that the expenditures on the constituent items of leafy vegetables are the same; in other words, this assumption means that
none of the constituent items of leafy vegetables would show any
preferred importance in consumption. Such a process of subdivision appears to be realizable in practice. At least, the extent to which the assumption is realizable may be considered to
be sufficient for all practical purposes.

5.3. AN UNBIASED ESTIMATE

Let the entire consumption be divided into g divisions,
and let the number of items in the ith division be N_i ($i = $
1, 2, ..., g). This N_i may be large, but it is finite. If
w_i is the weight corresponding to the ith division, the cost
of living index, under the assumption, is given by

$$R = \frac{\sum_{j=1}^{N_1} r_{1j}(w_1/N_1) + \sum_{j=1}^{N_2} r_{2j}(w_2/N_2) + \cdots + \sum_{j=1}^{N_g} r_{gj}(w_g/N_g)}{N_1(w_1/N_1) + N_2(w_2/N_2) + \cdots + N_g(w_g/N_g)}$$

$$(5.3)$$

where r_{ij} is the price relative of the jth item in the ith
division (stratum). In (5.3), the denominator is equal to
$\Sigma_i \, w_i = 1$; R takes account of all items consumed and is the
expanded form of (5.2), showing the price relatives by divisions.

Let us now choose at random n_i from N_i items of the ith
division. These $n \, (= \Sigma_i \, n_i)$ price relatives lead to the best
and unbiased estimate of R.

Let $r_{ij}(w_i/N_i) = S_{ij}$. With this substitution, R reduces
to

$$\sum_i \sum_j S_{ij}$$

Since w_i/N_i is constant over the ith division, S_{ij} can be
considered as a random variable in the ith division, just as
is r_{ij}. The estimating function for R is constructed as

$$\frac{\sum_{k=1}^{n_1} r_{1k}(w_1/n_1) + \sum_{k=1}^{n_2} r_{2k}(w_2/n_2) + \cdots + \sum_{k=1}^{n_g} r_{gk}(w_g/n_g)}{n_1(w_1/n_1) + n_2(w_2/n_2) + \cdots + n_g(w_g/n_g)}$$

$$= \sum_{k=1}^{n_1} r_{1k} \frac{w_1}{n_1} + \sum_{k=1}^{n_2} r_{2k} \frac{w_2}{n_2} + \cdots + \sum_{k=1}^{n_g} r_{gk} \frac{w_g}{n_g} \qquad (5.4)$$

since

$$n_1 \frac{w_1}{n_1} + n_2 \frac{w_2}{n_2} + \cdots + n_g \frac{w_g}{n_g} = 1$$

The first term of (5.4) can be written as

$$\sum_{k=1}^{n_1} r_{1k} \frac{w_1}{n_1} \frac{N_1}{N_1} = \frac{N_1}{n_1} \sum_{k=1}^{n_1} r_{1k} \frac{w_1}{N_1} = \frac{N_1}{n_1} \sum_{k=1}^{n_1} S_{1k} \qquad (5.5)$$

The expectation of (5.5) given by

$$E \frac{N_1}{n_1} \sum_{k=1}^{n_1} S_{lk} = \sum_{j=1}^{N_1} S_{lj}$$

Taking successively the expectation of each of the g terms of (5.4) we find that the expectation of (5.4) is R. Hence, (5.4) is an unbiased estimate of R. In each of these divisions, the sum of products of the price relatives and the weights is substituted, in the estimate, by the product of the average of price relatives of the sampled items and the weight of the division.

The variance of the first term of (5.4) is given by

$$\frac{w_1^2}{n_1^2} \frac{N_1 - n_1}{N_1 - 1} n_1 \sigma_1^2 \quad \text{(without replacement)}$$

$$= w_1^2 \frac{N_1 - n_1}{N_1 - 1} \frac{\sigma_1^2}{n_1}$$

where σ_1^2 is the variance of r_{lk}.

Calculating the variance of each of these terms as above, we can write the variance for (5.4) as

$$\sum_i \frac{N_i - n_i}{N_i - 1} \frac{\sigma_i^2 w_i^2}{n_i} \tag{5.6}$$

5.4.   OPTIMUM ALLOCATION

For estimate (5.4) to be the best, (5.6) has to be the minimum. The cost of including all the $n = \Sigma_i n_i$ items can be taken as

$$C = \sum_i n_i c_i \tag{5.7}$$

where c_i is the cost per item of the ith division (stratum). Expression (5.6) can now be minimized with respect to n_i along with restraint (5.7) after the Neyman method [51]. Using the usual method of Lagrangian multipliers, we get

$$\lambda c_i = \frac{w_i^2}{n_i^2} \sigma_i^2 \frac{N_i}{N_i - 1}$$

for all i values, where λ is a constant. Neglecting -1 compared with N_i, the above reduces to[*]

$$\lambda c_i = \frac{w_i^2}{n_i^2} \sigma_i^2$$

Hence,

$$n_i = \frac{\sigma_i w_i}{\sqrt{\lambda c_i}}$$

The c_i values can be taken as equal, so that $c_i = c_2 = \cdots = c_i = c$. With this assumption,

$$n_i = \frac{\sigma_i w_i}{\sqrt{\lambda c}} = \frac{\sigma_i w_i}{k}$$

where $k = \sqrt{\lambda c}$. Remembering that $\Sigma_i n_i = n$, we calculate the value of k as $\Sigma_i \sigma_i w_i / n$. Hence,

---

[*]If the notation is changed from σ^2 to s^2, where $s^2 = \Sigma(y_i - \bar{Y})^2/(N-1)$ and $\sigma^2 = \Sigma(y_i - \bar{Y})^2/N$, $\bar{Y}$, the mean of the finite population of size N, we will get $\lambda c_i = \omega_i^2 s_i^2 / n_i^2$. With this change, it is not necessary to make the assumption that -1 is negligible compared to N to get this form for λc_i. S_i may be substituted for σ_i in all these expressions.

$$n_i = \frac{n\sigma_i w_i}{\sum_i \sigma_i w_i}$$

That is, in order that the variance estimate (5.4) be the minimum, n has to be divided in the i divisions (strata) in proportion to σw.

5.5. ERROR VARIANCE

Neglecting -1 compared with N_i, variance (5.6) can be reduced to the form

$$\sum_i \frac{N_i - n_i}{N_i} \frac{\sigma_i^2 w_i^2}{n_i}$$

$$= \sum_i \sigma_i^2 w_i^2 \left(\frac{1}{n_i} - \frac{1}{N_i} \right) \tag{5.8}$$

If $1/N_i$ is neglected, since w_i is a fraction and N_i is large, expression (5.8) reduces to

$$\sum_i \frac{\sigma_i^2 w_i^2}{n_i}$$

Notice that the whole weight of the composite commodity is involved only in the estimate and the variance of the index. This makes the formulas practicable.

5.6. REDUCTION OF THE UNBIASED ESTIMATE TO AGGREGATIVE FORM

Expressed in full, Laspeyres' aggregative formula takes the form

$$\frac{\sum_i \sum_j p_{ij}^1 q_{ij}^0}{\sum_i \sum_j p_{ij}^0 q_{ij}^0} \tag{5.9}$$

With these notations,

$$w_i = \frac{\Sigma_j \; p_{ij}^O q_{ij}^O}{\Sigma_i \; \Sigma_j \; p_{ij}^O q_{ij}^O}$$

Under the stated assumption of equality of importance (expenditure) of the constituent items,

$$p_{i1}^O q_{i1}^O = p_{i2}^O q_{i2}^O = \cdots = p_{iN_i}^O q_{iN_i}^O = e_i^O \quad (\text{say})$$

Hence, $w_i = N_i e_i^O / \Sigma_i \; \Sigma_j \; p_{ij}^O q_{ij}^O$. If we substitute the value of w_i in (5.4), cancel the p^O terms, and keep in mind the fact that e_i^O can be any one of the quantities $p_{ij}^O q_{ij}^O$ (j = 1, 2, ..., N_i), (5.4) reduces to

$$\frac{\Sigma_i \; (N_i/n_i) \; \Sigma_{k=1}^{n_i} \; p_{ik}^1 q_{ik}^O}{\Sigma_i \; \Sigma_j \; p_{ij}^O q_{ij}^O} \tag{5.10}$$

In the numerator of (5.10), the aggregate cost of the n_i sampled constituent items of the ith composite commodity is multiplied by N_i/n_i and then such products are aggregated. Expression (5.10) is obviously an unbiased estimate of (5.9).

5.7.   IMPLICATIONS OF A PREVALENT PRACTICE

If, instead of assuming the equality of importance (expenditure) of the constituent items, we assume the equality of the quantities q_{ij}^O of the ith composite commodity, the average price of the ith composite commodity in the period O can be taken as $\Sigma_j \; p_{ij}^O q_{ij}^O / \Sigma_j \; q_{ij}^O = \Sigma_j \; p_{ij}^O / N_i$. An unbiased estimate of this average is the sample average $\Sigma_k \; p_{ik}^O / n_i$, in which n_i items have been sampled. The estimate of the index is then expressed as

$$\sum_i r_i w_i = \sum_i \frac{\sum_k p_{ik}^1/n_i}{\sum_k p_{ik}^0/n_i} \, w_i \tag{5.11}$$

where $w_i = \sum_j p_{ij}^0 q_{ij}^0 / \sum_i \sum_j p_{ij}^0 q_{ij}^0$.

Another noticeable implication is that the price relative has been substituted by the ratio of two average prices.

If we equate $\sum_k p_{ik}^0/n_i$ with $\sum_j p_{ij}^0/N_i$ and remember the fact that the q_{ij}^0 terms are equal, (5.11) reduces to (5.10).

In (5.11), the price relative to the ith composite commodity, obtained as the ratio of the arithmetic averages of the n_i prices in the periods 1 and 0, is weighted with the weight w_i. The variance of (5.11) is approximated as

$$\sum_i \frac{N_i - n_i}{N_i - 1} \, \frac{\sigma_i^2 w_i^2}{n_i} \tag{5.12}$$

where $\sigma_i^2 = V(p_{ik}^1/p_{ik}^0)$, that is, the variance of a price relative. The variance of (5.11) can also be approximated by any other standard formula relevant to a ratio estimate.

5.8. SAMPLING ERRORS AND STUDIES ON PRECISION

This author has considered different types of sampling in the construction of cost of living index numbers and has compared the errors under the different sampling procedures. These studies also include the treatment of composite commodities in the perspective of bringing overall precision to cost of living index numbers. The interested reader may refer to refs. [7,9, 11,12,15, and 16] for details.

5.9. WEIGHTS OF CONSTITUENT ITEMS OF COMPOSITE COMMODITIES USUALLY UNKNOWN IN PRACTICE

Weights are usually determined from a family budget survey. The questionnaire of such an inquiry generally provides for entries of expenditure on composite commodities. Thus, weights of composite commodities only can be computed. Because it is not possible, for practical reasons, to know the expenditure on the constituent items of a composite commodity individually, the weights for the constituent items remain unknown. Consequently, a formula must be used in which the weight of a composite commodity as a whole, rather than the weights of the constituent items, is involved.

The precision of the calculated index largely depends how a composite commodity is composed and what items are included in the price collection schedule. A group of items (composite commodity) may consist of a large number (finite) of constituent items, each of which is associated with a price relative. Because it is impracticable to include all the constituent items of a composite commodity in the construction, the construction must be confined to a sample of the constituent items. The next step is to determine how the sample can best be drawn, consistent with the condition that only the weight of a composite commodity as a whole is known. We have seen how, under a simplifying assumption, an unbiased estimate of the index can be found and that this estimate contains the weight of a composite commodity as a whole. Such an estimate would therefore serve the purpose.

APPENDIXES

DIFFERENTIAL DEFINITION OF THE INDEX AND ITS DERIVATION

A brief account of the ingenious derivation of the index
number formula by F. Divisia [28,29] will be presented here.
His work was extended by R. Roy [52]. The interpretation inherent in the derivation assists in appreciating the relative
positions of the known formulas. The derivation is based on a
differential method. It depends on the admissibility of expressing the cost Σ pq as a product of two factors P and Q
in the form

$$PQ = \Sigma \, pq \qquad\qquad (A.1)$$

where P represents the general price level and Q denotes
the total physical volume. In the present context, we are interested in P which would measure the level of consumer prices.
Since a change in cost may result from either a change in prices
or a change in quantities consumed, Eq. (A.1) can be written
in differential form as

$$P \, dQ + Q \, dP = \Sigma \, (p \, dq + q \, dp) \qquad\qquad (A.2)$$

Dividing (A.2) by PQ, we get

$$\frac{dQ}{Q} + \frac{dP}{P} = \frac{\Sigma\, p\, dq}{PQ} + \frac{\Sigma\, q\, dp}{PQ}$$

$$= \frac{\Sigma\, p\, dq}{\Sigma\, pq} + \frac{\Sigma\, q\, dp}{\Sigma\, pq} \qquad (A.3)$$

Separating $(A.3)$ into two differentials, the differential in price and the differential in quantity, we get

$$\frac{dQ}{Q} = \frac{\Sigma\, p\, dq}{\Sigma\, pq}, \quad \frac{dP}{P} = \frac{\Sigma\, q\, dp}{\Sigma\, pq} \qquad (A.4)$$

Each of Eqs. $(A.4)$ is a differential equation. We are interested in $dP/P = \Sigma\, q\, dp/\Sigma\, pq$, the solution of which gives the price index. The other relates to quantity and, when integrated, gives a quantity index. In the former, quantity is assumed to be constant and, in the latter, price is assumed to be constant. Assuming that the quantities q consumed in the period compared are proportional to those consumed in the base period 0, that is, assuming $q = \lambda q_0$, we get the differential in price as

$$\frac{dP}{P} = \frac{\Sigma\, q\, dp}{\Sigma\, pq} = \frac{\Sigma\, \lambda q_0\, dp}{\Sigma\, \lambda pq_0} = \frac{\Sigma\, q_0\, dp}{\Sigma\, pq_0} = \frac{d(\Sigma\, pq_0)}{\Sigma\, pq_0} \qquad (A.5)$$

where P and p are the variables, and $q = \lambda q_0 = $ constant. Integrating $(A.5)$, we get

$$\log P = \log(\Sigma\, pq_0) + c \qquad (A.6)$$

where c is an arbitrary constant the value of which has to be determined from initial conditions. We next suppose that the prices in the base period are p_0 and that P_0 is the corresponding index (i.e., the price level in the base period 0). From $(A.6)$, we get

$$\log \frac{P}{P_0} = \log \frac{\Sigma\, pq_0}{\Sigma\, p_0 q_0}$$

or

$$\frac{P}{P_0} = \frac{\Sigma\, pq_0}{\Sigma\, p_0 q_0} \qquad\qquad\qquad (A.7)$$

Equation (A.7) is easily recognized as Laspeyres' formula. In a similar manner, Paasche's index can be derived from the same differential equation by setting q equal to λq_1, where q_1 represents the quantities consumed in the period compared. The ideal formula of Irving Fisher can also be deduced from the same differential equation. If the summation in the numerator of (A.5) is broken up into two summations denoted by Σ_1 and Σ_2, we get

$$\frac{dP}{P} = \frac{\Sigma_1\, q\, dp + \Sigma_2\, q\, dp}{\Sigma\, pq} = \frac{\Sigma_1\, q\, dp}{\Sigma\, pq} + \frac{\Sigma_2\, q\, dp}{\Sigma\, pq}$$

$$= \frac{\Sigma_1\, q\, dp}{\Sigma_1\, pq}\, \frac{\Sigma_1\, pq}{\Sigma\, pq} + \frac{\Sigma_2\, q\, dp}{\Sigma_2\, pq}\, \frac{\Sigma_2\, pq}{\Sigma\, pq}$$

$$= \frac{\Sigma_1\, q\, dp}{\Sigma_1\, pq}\, \alpha_1 + \frac{\Sigma_2\, q\, dp}{\Sigma_2\, pq}\, \alpha_2 \qquad\qquad (A.8)$$

where, obviously, $\alpha_1 + \alpha_2 = 1$.

Setting $\Sigma_1\, q\, dp / \Sigma_1\, pq$ equal to dP_1/P_1 and $\Sigma_2\, q\, dp / \Sigma_2\, pq$ equal to dP_2/P_2, and taking $\alpha_1 = \alpha_2 = 1/2$, we reduce (A.8) to the form

$$\frac{dP}{P} = \frac{1}{2}\left(\frac{dP_1}{P_1} + \frac{dP_2}{P_2}\right) \qquad\qquad (A.9)$$

The constant q is at our disposal and can be taken as λq_0 and λq_1, respectively, in $\Sigma_1\, q\, dp / \Sigma_1\, pq$ $(= dP_1/P_1)$ and $\Sigma_2\, q\, dp / \Sigma_2\, pq$ $(= dP_2/P_2)$.

Integrating (A.9) we get (omitting the subscripts of Σ),

$$\log P = \frac{1}{2} \log(\Sigma\ pq_0)(\Sigma\ pq_1) + d \tag{A.10}$$

Let the prices in the base period be p_0 and the corresponding index be P_0. Then, from (A.10) we get

$$\log P_0 = \frac{1}{2} \log(\Sigma\ p_0 q_0)(\Sigma\ p_0 q_1) + d \tag{A.11}$$

Substituting in (A.10) the value of d obtained from (A.11), we get

$$\log \frac{P}{P_0} = \frac{1}{2} \log \frac{\Sigma\ pq_0\ \Sigma\ pq_1}{\Sigma\ p_0 q_0\ \Sigma\ p_0 q_1} \tag{A.12}$$

or $P/P_0 = (LP)^{1/2}$, where L and P are Laspeyres' and Paasche's formulas, respectively. The above will be recognized as the ideal formula of Irving Fisher. In Eqs. (A.7) and (A.12), the subscripts of p are dropped. The prices p refer to the period of comparison.

A COMMENT ON THE
CONSTRUCTION OF PRICE INDEX NUMBERS*

B.1.   INTRODUCTION

Ruderman [53] drew attention to a point that is often neglected in the construction of cost of living index (CLI) numbers. Usually, the mean-of-relatives form (according to notations used by him)

$$\frac{\Sigma(p_1/p_0) \; p_0 q_0}{\Sigma \; p_0 q_0} \qquad\qquad (B.1)$$

is used in the construction of CLI numbers. If the p_0 of
(p_1/p_0) and the p_0 of $p_0 q_0$ are cancelled out, (B.1) reduces
to the aggregative form of Laspeyres, which is

$$\frac{\Sigma \; p_1 q_0}{\Sigma \; p_0 q_0} \qquad\qquad (B.2)$$

---

*Taken from K.S. Banerjee [8].

Ruderman points out that the transformation of (B.1) to (B.2) is not possible because the p_0 elements in (p_1/p_0) and $p_0 q_0$ are different. The prices p_1 and p_0 of the price relative (p_1/p_0) are market (store) prices, whereas the values of p_0 implicit in the expenditure weights $p_0 q_0$ are obtained from family living studies. The latter price p_0 relates to a class of commodities and represents the average price of all goods in the class actually purchased at all prices actually paid in all markets patronized. The two p_0 elements are therefore different and cannot, as such, cancel out. Using the subscript s to identify market (store) prices and f to denote prices obtained from family budget studies, we can express the weighted mean of relatives by

$$\frac{\Sigma \; (p_{s1}/p_{s0}) \; p_{f0} q_0}{\Sigma \; p_{f0} q_0} \tag{B.3}$$

Indicating the difference between p_{f0} and p_{s0} by some ratio a such that $p_{f0} = a p_{s0}$, Ruderman calculates, for some commodities, the values of a that have been found to be different from unity.

B.2.   SUGGESTED METHOD OF COMPUTING THE PRICE RELATIVE

In some institutions engaged in the construction of the CLI, the prices p_1 and p_0 of the price relative (p_1/p_0) are weighted average prices, where quantities sold in the market are the weights. It is shown in this section that the average price p_0 weighted as such is an unbiased estimate of

p_{fo} under certain reasonable assumptions. If this is so, the deviation of a from unity is a matter of sampling fluctuation.

Using an example, let us explain what we mean by the average price weighted with the quantities sold in the market and how such average prices claim to meet the point raised by Ruderman. In the major group food, leafy vegetables, for instance, appear as an item of consumption. Usually, one weight is available for the item leafy vegetables, which is its proportion of expenditure to total expenditure (or to expenditure on food, if the construction of the CLI is to be completed in the first stage individually for each of the major groups and in the second stage for all the major groups combined).

There may be, say, sixty or more varieties of leafy vegetables consumed by the class of families for which the CLI is constructed. The expenditure $p_0 q_0$ on this item, which is obtained from family budget studies, is the total expenditure incurred on all sixty varieties.

When monthly indexes are required, the price-reporting agents, while collecting prices on several days of the months from all the markets (or a sample of markets) patronized, also record the volume of sales against the items priced. Usually, the volume of sales (or projected sales) for the whole market day is recorded against the item. Collecting information on the quantities sold is possible with respect to nearly all the food items, including vegetables, fish, meat, eggs, fruit, etc. Prices are then averaged with quantities as weights. Bear in mind that here the prices are weighted with quantities sold in the market, while the quantities q_0 of $p_0 q_0$ are quantities consumed in the family. There is therefore a difference between the two.

B.3. COMPARISON WITH RUDERMAN'S AVERAGE PRICE

Let there be M varieties of the item under consideration (say, leafy vegetables) and let there be N families from which budgets were collected in the base period; also let q_{ij}^0 (≥ 0) be the quantity of the ith variety consumed by the jth family. Then, using the superscript 0 for the sake of convenience,

$$p_0 q_0 = \sum_i \sum_j p_i^0 q_{ij}^0 \tag{B.4}$$

Let us express $p_0 q_0$ in the form $\bar{p}_0 Q_0$, where $\bar{p}_0 = C_0/Q_0$, C_0 is the right-hand side of (B.4), and $Q_0 = \sum_i \sum_j q_{ij}^0$. That is, $\bar{p}_0$ is the weighted average price, where the quantities consumed in the family are the weights. If the price p_0 in $p_0 q_0$ could be expressed as a single price figure, it would be the same as $\bar{p}_0$. This $\bar{p}_0$ is notationally equivalent to p_{f0} of Ruderman.

If it were possible to collect the quotations of prices together with the quantities purchased by the families with respect to all the M varieties sold in all the markets patronized by a class of people (say, the working class in an industrial area in which the markets may be localized) on all the market days, it would be possible to secure, for each variety, the total quantity consumed by the N families. In that case, the weighted average price, where the quantities sold in the market are the weights would be exactly the same as p_{f0}. However, this is impracticable. Usually a selection is made of m varieties out of M, and quotations of prices and quantities are collected on some of the market days (if monthly indexes are constructed). Probably only a fraction of the N families makes purchases on those market days.

Let $\hat{Q}_i$ (dropping the superscript 0) be the total quantity of the ith variety sold, and let $\hat{Q}$ be the total quantity of all the m varieties sold. Multiplying $\hat{Q}_i$ by p_i^0, we get $p_i^0 \hat{Q}_i$, which is the total value of sales of the ith variety.

Written in full, $\hat{Q}_i$ is equal to

$$q'_{i1} + q'_{i2} + \cdots + q'_{in_i}$$

where q'_{ik} ($i = 1, 2, \ldots, m$; $k = 1, 2, \ldots, n_i$) is the quantity of the ith variety purchased by the kth family. Written in full, the market transactions with respect to all the m varieties are

$$
\begin{aligned}
\sum_{i=1}^{m} p_i^O \hat{Q}_i = \; & p_1^O(q'_{11} + q'_{12} + \cdots + q'_{1n_1}) \\
& + p_2^O(q'_{21} + q'_{22} + \cdots + q'_{2n_2}) \\
& \quad \vdots \qquad\quad \vdots \qquad\qquad \vdots \\
& + p_i^O(q'_{i1} + q'_{i2} + \cdots + q'_{in_i}) \\
& \quad \vdots \qquad\quad \vdots \qquad\qquad \vdots \\
& + p_m^O(q'_{m1} + q'_{m2} + \cdots + q'_{mn_m})
\end{aligned}
\tag{B.5}
$$

Equation (B.5) can be expressed in the form

$$\sum_{i=1}^{m} p_i^O \hat{Q}_i = \hat{p}_O \hat{Q} \tag{B.6}$$

where $\hat{p}_O = \hat{C}_O / \hat{Q}$, and $\hat{C}_O$ is the left-hand side of (B.5). Thus, $\hat{p}_O$ is the weighted average price, where quantities sold are the weights.

The above quantities q'_{ik} ($i = 1, 2, \ldots, m$; $k = 1, 2, \ldots, n_i$) have their equals in the quantities q_{ij}^O ($i = 1, 2, \ldots, M$; $j = 1, 2, \ldots, N$) of (B.4), but it is not known which of the former is equal to which of the latter.

Any of the N families can make a transaction with respect to any of the varieties on any of the market days. The occurrence of q'_{ik} can therefore be taken as random.

Since p_i^O is constant over the ith variety and since the occurrence of q_{ik}' is random,

$$p_i^O q_{ik}' = x_{ik}, \quad i = 1, 2, \ldots, m; \ k = 1, 2, \ldots, n_i$$

can be taken as a random variable in the ith variety. Under these assumptions, the total of the market transactions can be taken as the result of a two-stage sampling in which m varieties are chosen, in the first stage, out of M, and n_i transactions are made in the ith variety. The unbiased estimate of (B.4) is then given by

$$\frac{M}{m} \sum_i \frac{N}{n_i} \sum_k x_{ik} \tag{B.7}$$

The n_i's are not known. It may not, perhaps, be unreasonable to assume equality of the n_i's. Let $n_i = n$; (B.7) then reduces to $K \sum_i \sum_k x_{ik}$, where $K = MN/mn$. That is,

$$C_O = E\left(K \sum_i \sum_k x_{ik} \right) = KE(\hat{C}_O)$$

where E stands for mathematical expectation. In the same way it can be shown that

$$Q_O = E\left(K \sum_i \sum_k q_{ik}' \right) = KE(\hat{Q})$$

Now, if it is assumed that

$$E(\hat{p}_O) = E\left(\frac{\hat{C}_O}{\hat{Q}} \right) = \frac{E(\hat{C}_O)}{E(\hat{Q})}$$

then

$$E(\hat{p}_O) = \frac{C_O}{Q_O} = \bar{p}_O$$

that is, $\hat{p}_0$ is an unbiased estimate of $\bar{p}_0$, which is the same as p_{f0} of Ruderman.

In Chapter 1, a weighted average price was recommended as the representative price for a composite commodity, where the weights with which the prices are to be averaged are quantities sold of the constituent items of the composite commodity. The above is a justification for such a recommendation.

CHOICE OF CONVERSION FACTOR IN THE
DERIVATION OF AN INDEX OF A DISCONTINUED SERIES*

C.1. INTRODUCTION

When an older series of index numbers is discontinued and
a new series is started with a new weight base, a factor of
equivalence, usually called a conversion factor, is calculated
for that period of time from which the new series is begun.
This conversion factor is utilized to derive a series of index
numbers approximating the discontinued series. It may, at
times, be imperative to know what the values of the older series
would have been had the series not been discontinued. Judged
in the light of this requirement, a conversion factor would be
considered the best if it afforded the closest agreement with
the discontinued series. The aim of this appendix is to dis-
cuss the merits of different conversion factors.

---

*Taken from K.S. Banerjee [13].

C.2.   THE THREE CONVERSION FACTORS

Let us denote the base period for the older series as the period 0 and the base period for the new series as the period t. Then, by Laspeyres' formula, the index for the period t with reference to the base 0 is

$$L_{0t} = 100 \, \frac{\Sigma \, p_t q_0}{\Sigma \, p_0 q_0} \qquad\qquad (C.1)$$

Since we know the weights for the period t, we can calculate the index for this period by Paasche's formula as well. This is given by

$$P_{0t} = 100 \, \frac{\Sigma \, p_t q_t}{\Sigma \, p_0 q_t} \qquad\qquad (C.2)$$

From (C.1) and (C.2), we also know the index by Fisher's formula, as given by

$$F_{0t} = \sqrt{L_{0t} P_{0t}}$$

Three conversion factors, $L_{0t}/100$, $P_{0t}/100$, and $F_{0t}/100$, are therefore, possible.

C.3.   DISCUSSION

The index for the period u in the new series, by Laspeyres' formula, is

$$100 \, \frac{\Sigma \, p_u q_t}{\Sigma \, p_t q_t}$$

which we denote by X, while the index for the same period u in the older series, by Laspeyres' formula, is

$$100 \frac{\Sigma \; p_u q_0}{\Sigma \; p_0 q_0}$$

which we denote by Y.

Our problem is to derive Y from X. The index numbers derived by the three conversion factors are

$$100 \frac{\Sigma \; p_u q_t}{\Sigma \; p_t q_t} \frac{\Sigma \; p_t q_0}{\Sigma \; p_0 q_0}$$

which we denote by XL

$$100 \frac{\Sigma \; p_u q_t}{\Sigma \; p_t q_t} \frac{\Sigma \; p_t q_t}{\Sigma \; p_0 q_t}$$

which we denote by XP

$$100 \frac{\Sigma \; p_u q_t}{\Sigma \; p_t q_t} \sqrt{\frac{\Sigma \; p_t q_0}{\Sigma \; p_0 q_0} \frac{\Sigma \; p_t q_t}{\Sigma \; p_0 q_t}}$$

which we denote by $X(LP)^{1/2}$. It is now necessary to find which of the three index numbers given above is nearest to Y.

Let $a = XL - Y$, $b = XP - Y$, and $c = X(LP)^{1/2} - Y$. If both a and b are positive, c is also positive. If both a and b are negative, c is also negative. If a is positive and b is negative, c is either positive or negative. The possibility of a being negative and b positive can be ignored because L is unlikely to be less than P. The situations that do arise and the conclusion in each case are outlined below. The results are derived mainly from the relations $(LP)^{1/2} > P$ or $(LP)^{1/2} < L$, which imply that the geometric mean of two numbers lies between the numbers.

Situation 1 (Fig. C.1).
Let both a and b be positive.
Then, $P_{Ot}/100$ is better than
$L_{Ot}/100$ as a conversion factor,
and $F_{Ot}/100$ is also better
than $L_{Ot}/100$. Of the two conversion factors $P_{Ot}/100$ and
$F_{Ot}/100$, $P_{Ot}/100$ is better than $F_{Ot}/100$.

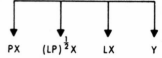

Situation 2 (Fig. C.2).
Let both a and b be negative.
Then, $L_{Ot}/100$ is better than
$P_{Ot}/100$ as a conversion factor,
and $F_{Ot}/100$ is also better
than $P_{Ot}/100$. Of the two factors
$L_{Ot}/100$ and $F_{Ot}/100$, $L_{Ot}/100$ is better than $F_{Ot}/100$.

Situation 3.* Let a be positive and b negative. Let
$a < -b$. It can easily be shown that $LP = [\frac{1}{2}(L+P)]^2 - [\frac{1}{2}(L-P)]^2$
Hence

$$(LP)^{1/2} < \frac{L + P}{2}$$

$$(LP)^{1/2}X < (\frac{L + P}{2})X$$

$$(LP)^{1/2}X - Y < (\frac{L + P}{2})X - Y$$

$$< \frac{LX - Y}{2} + \frac{PX - X}{2}$$

$$\therefore \qquad c < \frac{a + b}{2}$$

Thus, if $a < -b$, then c must be negative.

---

*The algebraic portion of the exposition in Situation 3
is taken from Dr. D. G. Beech (by correspondence).

Let us look at situation 3 geometrically (Fig. C.3).

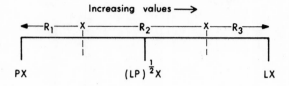

For situation 3 to hold, Y must be depicted as falling some-
where on the line joining PX to LX, the values being plotted
to scale. The vertical dashed lines bisect the two segments
into which $(LP)^{1/2}X$ divides the line. If Y falls in region
R_1, then PX is the best estimate; if Y falls in region R_2,
then $(LP)^{1/2}X$ is the best estimate; if Y falls in region R_3,
then LX is the best estimate; $(LP)^{1/2}X$ is never the worst
estimate. Now,

$$R_2 = \frac{(LP)^{1/2}X - PX}{2} + \frac{LX - (LP)^{1/2}X}{2}$$

$$= \frac{LX - PX}{2}$$

So if Y can fall on any part of the whole line LX - PX with
equal probability, it has a 50% chance of falling in region R_2.
Hence, if our assumptions about the location of Y are correct,
$(LP)^{1/2}X$ will be the best estimate on half of the possible
occasions in situation 3.

C.4. CONCLUSION

In situations 1 and 2, either the Laspeyres or the Paasche
conversion factor will be the best, and the conversion factor
based on Fisher's ideal index will occupy an intermediate
position. In situation 3, the conversion factor based on

Fisher's index may be the best or may occupy an intermediate
position. We do not, of course, know the relative frequencies
of these situations and subsituations; nevertheless, there are
grounds for recommending Fisher's index as the basis for the
conversion factor, because it occupies either the intermediate
or the best position. It is never the worst factor, whereas
the Paasche or the Laspeyres factor may be. In practice, the
conversion factor from Laspeyres' index is usually adopted,
although no additional data are required for the use of the
conversion factor based on Fisher's ideal index.

APPENDIX D

PRECISION IN CONSTRUCTING
COST OF LIVING INDEX NUMBERS*

D.1.   INTRODUCTION

Although much attention has been drawn to the problem of
securing the true index (TI) in the context of constructing cost
of living index (CLI) numbers and formulas have been evolved
[32,45,64] for the purpose of constructing the true index, these
formulas do not appear to have been used much in practice. However, Laspeyres' base-weighted formula continues to be widely
used for approximating the CLI in spite of the fact that it is
known to overestimate the index.

D.2.   PRECISION NEGLECTED

Because it was necessary to construct the true index in
the precise estimation of the CLI and, instead, Laspeyres' formula is being used at the cost of precision, it would be only

_____
*Taken from K.S. Banerjee [12].

143

reasonable to at least ensure that Laspeyres' index is precisely
calculated. This aspect of precision does not appear to have
been paid the attention it deserves, so much so that it sometimes causes embarrassment when different organizations, calculating the CLI for the same area and the same economic stratum
of population, obtain different figures for the same index. The
difference in the figures for the same index could be at least
partly accounted for if the coverage (the sample, or the way
the sample is selected) and the error of estimation were made
available. In the absence of such information, controversies
arise, causing difficulty at administrative levels. With a
view to systematizing the study, the concept of standard error
in index number calculation was introduced in Chapter 5, where
it was shown that it is possible to calculate the standard error
for an estimated CLI under certain assumptions.

The purpose of this appendix is to show the extent of error
that might creep in through a nonjudicious computation of Laspeyres' index and to suggest measures of precaution. It is also
to demonstrate some principles that serve as guides in calculating Laspeyres' index on minimum price collection and minimum
computation.

The principles demonstrated here can be applied in general
to any index number formula which, or a part of which, is re-
ducible to the form of a weighted average of relatives.

D.3. LASPEYRES' FORMULA

Laspeyres' formula, $100 \sum_{i=1}^{N} p_{1i} q_{0i} / \sum_{i=1}^{N} p_{0i} q_{0i}$, is usually
adopted in routine practice in the reduced form, $\sum_i r_i w_i$, where
r_i $(= 100 p_{1i}/p_{0i})$ is the price relative of the ith consumption

item expressed as a percentage and w_i $(= p_{0i}q_{0i}/\Sigma_{i=1}^{N} p_{0i}q_{0i})$
is the weight of the ith item. Weight w_i is known and is
determined from family budgets such that $\Sigma_i w_i = 1$. The consumption items are usually grouped under major groups of consumption, and within each major group the items are again
grouped into subgroups that, in turn, may be either composite
commodities or single items. For each such subgroup, a price
relative is obtained, and such price relatives are averaged
with the corresponding weights.

The calculation of the index is generally completed in
two stages. It is first calculated for a major group, and then
the indexes for the major groups are combined into the overall
index. Usually, a subgroup is a composite commodity consisting
of numerous, although finite, constituent items. In that case,
the calculation has to be extended to the third stage, begin-
ning with the index for such a subgroup (composite commodity).

Without loss of generality, however, the calculation of
the index can be considered to be a two-stage process; that is,
the index is completed first for a composite commodity (subgroup), and then the indexes for the composite commodities (subgroups) are combined into the overall index. In that case,
Laspeyres' formula takes the form

$$\sum_{i=1}^{g} \sum_{j=1}^{N_i} r_{ij}w_{ij}, \quad i = 1, 2, \ldots, g; \quad j = 1, 2, \ldots, N_i$$

$$(D.1)$$

where r_{ij} and w_{ij} are, respectively, the price relative and
the weight of the jth constituent item of the ith composite
commodity, $\Sigma_i \Sigma_j w_{ij} = 1$, $\Sigma_j w_{ij} = w_i$, $\Sigma_i w_i = 1$, and $\Sigma_i N_i = N$.

D.4. A COMMON PRACTICE IN THE TREATMENT
OF A COMPOSITE COMMODITY

The weights of the individual constituent items of a composite commodity are not known in practice, because it is impracticable to determine the individual weights from a family budget inquiry. The information afforded by a family budget inquiry is the total weight for all the constituent items of the composite commodity. The prices of the constituent items are, of course, known.

Thus, r_{ij} of (D.1) is known, but w_{ij} is not. The absence of w_{ij} causes the difficulty in the precise estimation of the index, and this shortcoming appears to be mainly responsible for bringing into being divergent practices in the actual computation of the index.

To meet the situation of not knowing w_{ij}, some sort of price relative is calculated for the composite commodity as a whole, and then it is weighted with the total weight for the entire composite commodity. The price relative used in one such practice is the relative of the average prices in the base period 0 and in the given period 1. In this practice, the average price of the composite commodity is defined as the price averaged with the quantities of the constituent items sold in the market (see Appendix B).

With such a definition for the average price, the treatment of the composite commodity is in agreement, subject to sampling fluctuations, with the requirement of Laspeyres' index. However, there are certain assumptions involved in this practice that may not always be realizable for all types of composite commodities. These assumptions are as follows:

1. Acceptance of the definition for the average price of a composite commodity in the way it has been framed before.

2. Existence of the same supply pattern (relative supply) in both the base period 0 and the period of comparison 1.

Here, relative supply of a constituent item is taken to
mean the proportion of its supply to the total supply of the
composite commodity.

Assumption 1 can be accepted as reasonable in a given time
period only if the relative supply of the constituent items remains the same during the period. While this might hold good
with respect to many composite commodities, there may be some
composite commodities for which it might be quite wrong to make
this assumption. If, for those composite commodities, only the
cheaper of the constituent items appear for some reason in the
market in any period for sale, the average price of the composite commodity will be less than what it should be, and vice
versa.

If the validity of assumption 2 could be accepted at all,
it could perhaps be accepted to hold good during shorter intervals. At least, the probability of the assumption holding good
during shorter intervals of time would be higher than that during wider intervals. That this would be so is a limitation of
assumption 2.

D.5. A REASONABLE PROCEDURE AND OUTLOOK

A reasonable procedure is to calculate the price relatives
for n_i constituent items out of a total of N_i items constituting the composite commodity and to take an arithmetic
mean of the n_i price relatives, r_{ik} $(k = 1, 2, \ldots, n_i)$, in
order to calculate the index as

$$\sum_{i=1}^{g} \bar{r}_i^* w_i, \quad \text{where} \quad \bar{r}_i^* = \sum_{k=1}^{n_i} r_{ik}/n_i$$

The implications of this practice can be indicated as follows:

Let ρ_i be the correlation coefficient between r_{ij} and w_{ij}, and $w'_{ij} = w_{ij}/w_i$. Then, for the ith composite commodity, we have

$$\sum_j r_{ij}w'_{ij} = \sum_j r_{ij}/N_i + N_i\rho_i\sigma_{r_{ij}}\sigma_{w'_{ij}}$$

or

$$\sum_j r_{ij}w_{ij} = \bar{r}_i w_i + N_i\rho_i\sigma_{r_{ij}}\sigma_{w_{ij}} \tag{D.2}$$

where $\bar{r}_i = \Sigma_{j=1}^{N_i} r_{ij}/N_i$. If $\rho_i = 0$, we have $\Sigma_j r_{ij}w_{ij} = \bar{r}_i w_i$.

Under this condition, formula (D.1) reduces to $\Sigma_{i=1}^g \bar{r}_i w_i$. The condition $\rho_i = 0$, therefore dispenses with the necessity of knowing the individual weights w_{ij}.

The error variance of the estimate $\Sigma_i \bar{r}_i^* w_i$ can be derived as

$$\sum_i \frac{N_i - n_i}{N_i - 1} \frac{\sigma_i^2 w_i^2}{n_i} \tag{D.3}$$

where σ_i^2 is the variance of r_{ij} within i (see Chapter 5).

It should be remembered in this context that the individual weights of the constituent items can be pooled only if the correlation coefficient between the price relatives and the weights of the constituent items is zero.

If ρ_i is not equal to zero, this practice leads to an erroneous result. If ρ_i is either positive or negative for all i's, the errors are additive, resulting in a wide departure from what is being estimated. If, however, some of ρ_i values are positive and some are negative, the errors partly cancel out and, as a result, the magnitude of the added errors is less. If ρ_i is not equal to zero, its contribution to the error is $N_i\rho_i\sigma_{r_{ij}}\sigma_{w_{ij}} = N_i b_i \sigma_{r_{ij}}^2$, where b_i is the regression coefficient of w_{ij} on r_{ij}. Therefore, if each of the ρ_i values is not zero individually, we should have

$$\sum_{i=1}^{g} N_i b_i (\sigma_i)^2 = 0$$

so that no error is made. It appears that it would not be unreasonable to assume equality of the variances σ_i^2 from one
composite commodity to another. In that case, the above condition would reduce to

$$\sum_{i=1}^{g} N_i b_i = 0 \qquad\qquad (D.4)$$

For small values of ρ_i, the error involved may not be
much. Therefore, if the composite commodities could be so
taken as to ensure at least a small value for ρ_i, the practice
under consideration would be commendable. This practice has a
practical advantage in that it involves less effort than that
required to find a price averaged with quantities sold in the
market.

The illustrations in the next section show how the condition $\rho_i = 0$ can be utilized with advantage in constructing
the index on minimum computation.

D.6. NUMERICAL ILLUSTRATIONS

Table D.1 shows the calculation of the index on food. The
consumption of food has been divided into 25 composite commodities. Assuming that the index on food has been correctly calculated on these 25 composite commodities, we can use this numerical example to show how the composite commodities can be
further grouped so that the same index on food can be arrived

TABLE D.1

Price Relatives of Food Articles and Their Weights[a]

Items	Price relative	Weight (%)
1. Cereals	102	27.64
2. Cereal products	86	1.99
3. Wheat and wheat products	125	8.28
4. Other cereals and cereal products	95	0.72
5. Pulses	91	5.09
6. Edible oils	72	7.93
7. Vegetable oil	102	0.93
8. Salt	92	0.41
9. Spices	85	3.93
10. Sugar	93	4.67
11. Nonrefined sugar	123	0.56
12. Milk	101	3.44
13. Butter and whipped butter	95	0.71
14. Other milk products	96	0.63
15. Potatoes	62	4.13
16. Onions	155	0.69
17. Other nonleafy vegetables	57	8.31
18. Leafy vegetables	83	3.47
19. Fish	76	7.54
20. Meat	97	1.74
21. Eggs	80	0.39
22. Fruit	107	1.17
23. Tea and coffee	101	1.34
24. Refreshments and sweets	90	3.20
25. Other food articles	116	1.09
		100.00

[a]Index = 91.43.

at with fewer composite commodities.[*] Although some of these
suggested groupings, which have been made on the basis of zero
correlation, may not be practicable, these groupings are nonetheless used as illustrations to point out how the above result
can be exploited in computing the index on minimum effort.

The correlation coefficient between the 25 price relatives
and weights is -0.1390. The index on food calculated from the
25 composite commodities is 91.43, while a simple arithmetic
average of the price relatives is 95.28. Because there is a
negative correlation, the weighted index is less in magnitude
than the simple arithmetic average of the price relatives.

The 25 price relatives for the 25 composite commodities of
food have been plotted against the respective weights in Fig.
D.1. From the graph it can be readily determined as to which
of these 25 commodities can be further grouped. Five sets of
groupings have been suggested and the index for each has been
calculated, as shown at the bottom of each set in Table D.2.

The existence of criterion (4) is evident from the regression line being parallel to the axis of weights. Criteria (1),
(2), and (3) are only special cases for $\rho_i = 0$.

In determining the groups visually from the graph, use was
made of the following criteria: (1) equality of the weights,
or (2) equality of the price relatives, or (3) equality of
both weights and price relatives, or (4) $\rho_i = 0$.

The five-group set (Set I of Table D.2) has been marked
out in Fig. D.1, indicating which commodities have been pooled
together. The index is 91.52, while the index from the 25 commodities (groups) is 91.43. The agreement here is quite close.

---

[*]The pooling cannot be extended too far. Against this,
the magnitude of the error variance of the index estimated
through the pooling may be a limiting factor.

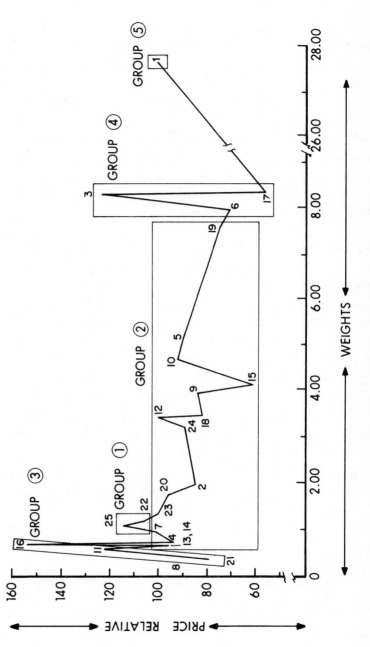

FIG. D.1 Grouping of consumption items.

The agreement is also sufficiently close in the other sets, except in set VI of Table D.2, which has been purposely indicated
because this kind of grouping is usually adopted in practice.
That is, items of a similar nature are grouped together. The
underlying assumption for this kind of grouping is perhaps the
equality of the price relatives giving zero value for the correlation coefficient. But this kind of grouping, as will be evident, may lead to erroneous results. The calculated index is
95.93, which differs widely from 91.43 and is nearly equal to
the index that would be obtained as a simple arithmetic average
of the price relatives of the 25 commodities. Adoption of a
course such as this is therefore tantamount to ignoring the
weights, even though the weights are relevant.

The principle can be further illustrated with reference
to Table D.3, where the indexes for the five conventionally
accepted major groups of consumption are shown along with the
overall CLI. Let the weights of the major groups 2, 3, and 4
be pooled and a simple arithmetic mean taken of the three indexes (price relatives) to correspond to the pooled weight of
these three major groups. These groups taken together will now
form one major group. In all, then, there will be three major
groups instead of five. The weighted average of these three
indexes (price relatives) is 95.6, which differs from the overall CLI by only 0.1.

D.7.   REMARKS

Set VI of Table D.2 demonstrates how nonjudicious grouping,
some kind of which is usually adopted in practice, might lead to
serious errors. The other illustrations point to the probable
good use that can be made of the basic principles in bringing
precision to the construction of index numbers.

TABLE D.2

Different Sets of Groups

Number of Groups	Sets					
	I	II	III	IV	V	VI
1	25, 22	25, 22	25, 22	25, 22	25, 22, 7	24, 25, 23, 22
2	24, 23, 20, 19, 18, 15, 14, 13, 12, 10, 9, 7, 5, 4, 2	24, 20, 18, 15, 14, 13, 12, 10, 9, 5, 4, 2	24, 18, 15, 12, 10, 9, 5, 2	24, 18, 15, 12, 10, 9, 5, 2	24	21, 20, 19
3	21, 16, 11, 8	23, 7	23, 7	23, 7	23	18, 17, 16, 15
4	17, 6, 3	21, 16, 11, 8	21, 16, 11, 8	21, 16, 11, 8	21, 16, 11, 8	14, 13, 12
5	1	19	20	20	20	11, 10
6		17, 3	19, 6	19	19	9, 8, 7, 6
7		6	17, 3	17, 3	18, 15, 12, 10, 9	5
8		1	14, 13, 4	14, 13, 4	17, 6, 3	4, 3, 2

8		1	14, 13, 4	14, 13, 4	17, 6, 3	4, 3, 2
9			1	6	14, 13, 4	1
10				1	5	
11					2	
12					1	
Index for food	91.52	91.94	91.26	91.25	91.40	95.93

TABLE D.3

CLI for a Month with Respect to a Town for a
Specific Expenditure Level

Major groups of consumption	For the specific expenditure level		
	Weight	Index	Weight × index
1. Food	58.55	91.4	5351.5
2. Clothing	5.37	106.5	571.9
3. Fuel and light	6.15	102.2	128.5
4. Housing	9.61	100.0	961.0
5. Miscellaneous	20.32	100.3	2038.1
All combined	100.00		95.5

CONNECTION OF THIEL'S BEST LINEAR AND KLOEK AND
DE WIT'S BEST LINEAR AVERAGE UNBIASED INDEX NUMBERS
WITH INDEX NUMBERS OBTAINED THROUGH THE FACTORIAL APPROACH

A set of quantities and a set of corresponding prices for
N commodities can be represented in the form of two $T \times N$
matrices as follows:

$$
Q = \begin{bmatrix} q_{11} & \cdots & q_{1N} \\ \vdots & & \vdots \\ q_{T1} & \cdots & q_{TN} \end{bmatrix}
\qquad
P = \begin{bmatrix} p_{11} & \cdots & p_{1N} \\ \vdots & & \vdots \\ p_{T1} & \cdots & p_{TN} \end{bmatrix}
$$

where T is the number of periods for which the quantities and
the prices are available. The cross-value matrix C is given
by C = PQ', where Q' is the transpose of Q. The elements
of C are the cross-value aggregates of the quantities of any
period priced at the prices of any period.

Theil [60] suggested that the price index and quantity index vectors p and q be found by minimizing the sum of squares
of the elements of the matrix E of cross-value discrepancies,
where

157

$$E = C - \underline{p}\underline{q}' \tag{E.1}$$

That is, $\underline{p}$ and $\underline{q}$ would be such that

$$\text{trace}(EE') = \text{trace}(E'E) = \text{minimum} \tag{E.2}$$

The minimization procedure leads finally to the necessary conditions as

$$(CC' - \underline{p}'\underline{p}\cdot\underline{q}'\underline{q}I)\underline{p} = 0 \tag{E.3}$$

$$(C'C - \underline{p}'\underline{p}\cdot\underline{q}'\underline{q}I)\underline{q} = 0 \tag{E.4}$$

From (E.3) and (E.4), it is clear that $\underline{p}$ and $\underline{q}$ are the characteristic vectors of CC' and $C'C$, respectively, and that CC' and $C'C$ have the same set of characteristic roots,

$$\underline{p}'\underline{p}\cdot\underline{q}'\underline{q} = \lambda^2 = \lambda \quad (\text{say})$$

In order to satisfy (E.2), the characteristic vectors corresponding to the largest root are taken.

To derive the indexes for a two-year period (i.e., when $T = 2$), the cross-value matrix is taken in the form

$$C = \begin{bmatrix} 1 & L_q \\ L_p & L_p L_q (1 + \eta) \end{bmatrix}$$

where $\Sigma_{i=1}^{N} p_{1i} q_{1i}$ is taken as unity, and L_p and L_q are Laspeyres' price and quantity indexes; η is defined as

$$P_p = L_p (1 + \eta) \tag{E.5}$$

where P_p is Paasche's price index and η is small.

From Eqs. (E.3) and (E.4), the price and quantity indexes are derived as

$$\pi \simeq L_p \left(1 + \eta \, \frac{L_q^2}{1 + L_q^2} \right) \quad \kappa \simeq L_q \left(1 + \eta \, \frac{L_p^2}{1 + L_p^2} \right) \tag{E.6}$$

In this derivation, higher powers of η have been neglected.

The above indexes are referred to as the best linear (B.L.) index numbers of Theil.

Kloek and De Wit [43] observed that Theil's B.L. indexes give an upward bias and that this is because the B.L. indexes do not satisfy the factor reversal test. In order to minimize the effect of this bias, Kloek and De Wit suggested that the sum of squares of the elements of E be minimized subject to the restraint

$$\text{trace}(E) = \text{trace}(C) - \underline{p}'\underline{q} = 0 \qquad\qquad (E.7)$$

Kloek and De Wit use restraint (E.7) because it removes the bias on the average. They call these indexes the best linear average unbiased (B.L.A.U.) index numbers.

After elaborate simplifications and neglecting higher powers of η, the price and quantity indexes $P_{\hat{\mu}}$ and $Q_{\hat{\mu}}$ are given by

$$P_{\hat{\mu}} = L_p \left[1 + \eta L_q \frac{L_q(1 + L_p^2) - (L_p - L_q)}{D + (L_p - L_q)^2} \right]$$

$$Q_{\hat{\mu}} = L_q \left[1 + \eta L_p \frac{L_p(1 + L_q^2) + (L_p - L_q)}{D + (L_p - L_q)^2} \right]$$

where $D = (1 + L_p^2)(1 + L_q^2)$.

We shall now trace the connection between the above indexes and those given by the factorial approach [20]. Denoting the periods as 0 and 1, we can write the cross-value matrix C as

$$C = \begin{bmatrix} a & aL_q = b \\ aL_p = c & aL_p L_q (1 + \eta) = d \end{bmatrix}$$

where $a = \Sigma\ p_0 q_0$, $b = \Sigma\ p_0 q_1$, $c = \Sigma\ p_1 q_0$, $d = \Sigma\ p_1 q_1$, and
$\eta = (ad - bc)/bc$.

Let P_0, P_1 and Q_0, Q_1 represent the price and the quantity vectors $\underline{p}$ and $\underline{q}$, respectively. We recall that, in order to make the indexes satisfy the factor reversal test on the average, Kloek and De Wit minimized the sum of squares of elements of the E matrix subject to the restraint

$$(a - P_0 Q_0) + (d - P_1 Q_1) = 0$$

In this context, we observe that it would be ideal if the indexes could possibly be found such that, separately,

$$a = P_0 Q_0 \quad b = P_0 Q_1$$
$$c = P_1 Q_0 \quad d = P_1 Q_1$$

This would reduce the matrix of cross-value discrepancies to zero.

It has been shown [20] that the price index P_1/P_0 and the quantity index Q_1/Q_0, obtained through the factorial approach, compare well with B.L.A.U. indexes. The connection between the two is as follows:

In this context, we take recourse to an orthogonal transformation. Let A be an orthogonal matrix given by

$$A = \frac{1}{\sqrt{2}} \begin{bmatrix} +1 & +1 \\ -1 & +1 \end{bmatrix}$$

Also, let $p^* = A\underline{p}$, $q^* = A\underline{q}$, $C^* = ACA'$, where A' is the transpose of A, and $\underline{p}$ and $\underline{q}$ are the price and the quantity vectors. Under this transformation, trace(EE'), the eigenvalues, and the eigenvectors remain invariant; C changes to $C^* = ACA'$ and is given by

$$C^* = \begin{bmatrix} M & \underline{Q} \\ \underline{P} & \underline{PQ} \end{bmatrix}$$

where $M = (a + b + c + d)/2$, $\underline{Q} = (-a + b - c + d)/2$, $\underline{P} = (-a - b + c + d)/2$, and $\underline{PQ} = (a - b - c + d)/2$. (Incidentally, in factorial experiments, M is usually written as $(a + b + c + d)/4$.)

Matrix E changes to E^*. If all the elements of E^* are equated to zero, we get the following identities:

(i) $(+P_0Q_0 + P_1Q_0 + P_0Q_1 + P_1Q_1)/2 = M$

(ii) $(-P_0Q_0 + P_1Q_0 - P_0Q_1 + P_1Q_1)/2 = \underline{P}$

(iii) $(-P_0Q_0 - P_1Q_0 + P_0Q_1 + P_1Q_1)/2 = \underline{Q}$

(iv) $(+P_0Q_0 - P_1Q_0 - P_0Q_1 + P_1Q_1)/2 = \underline{PQ}$

One wishes that the indexes could be found so that all the elements of E^* were zero. Instead, only two are equal to zero. That is, we adopt (ii) and (iii). The indexes $\pi = P_1/P_0$ and $\kappa = Q_1/Q_0$, shown below, are the same as given by Stuvel, satisfying the required factor reversal test:

$$\pi = \frac{L_p - L_q}{2} + \sqrt{\left(\frac{L_p - L_q}{2}\right)^2 + \frac{v_1}{v_0}}$$

$$\kappa = \frac{L_q - L_p}{2} + \sqrt{\left(\frac{L_q - L_p}{2}\right)^2 + \frac{v_1}{v_0}}$$

These indexes would bring in a considerable reduction in the sum of squares of the elements of the E^* matrix (cross-value discrepancy matrix), because two elements of the matrix (diagonals in the other direction) would be separately zero. In terms of the restraint of Kloek and De Wit, the above means

$$(a - P_0Q_0) - (d - P_1Q_1) = 0$$

instead of

$$(a - P_0Q_0) + (d - P_1Q_1) = 0$$

which is the restraint of Kloek and De Wit.

CONCLUSIONS AND RECOMMENDATIONS OF THE TENTH
INTERNATIONAL CONFERENCE OF LABOUR STATISTICIANS, 1962*

F.1. CONSUMER PRICE INDICES: SUMMARY OF THE CONCLUSIONS OF THE CONFERENCE

The Conference discussed in detail various problems in the
computation of consumer price indices, taking as a basis for
its deliberations the report which had been submitted by the
ILO on the subject [Report IV, reproduced as Part II of the
present document].

Finally, the Conference adopted unanimously a series of
recommendations.

The main points made during the discussions in the Conference are summarized in the following paragraphs.

The Conference first recognized the continuing validity of
the basic principles laid down by the Sixth International Conference of Labour Statisticians (Montreal, 1947) in its resolution concerning cost-of-living statistics, and in particular

---

*Reprinted from International Labour Office [37] by per-
mssion of the International Labour Office, as conveyed in
Dr. H.P. Lacroix's letter no. ST 01-1 of 6 November 1973.

the fact that the consumer price index is designed primarily to measure changes in the level of retail prices paid by consumers. It also confirmed the recommendations of the Sixth Conference that, if possible, separate index numbers should be compiled for different economic and social groups, geographical areas and different family types and that consideration should be given to establishing index numbers for economic and social, family and geographical groups other than those covered by the existing indices. In this connection, it was noted that existing consumer price indices rarely covered the rural population.

The Conference stressed the importance of public acceptance of consumer price indices. The maintenance of a modern consumer price index was an exceedingly complex operation, requiring high technical standards and well-trained statisticians, especially if index procedures were to cover all foreseeable contingencies in order to minimize the margin for subjective decisions required of officials responsible for the index. It was therefore necessary to give full publicity to the concepts, definitions and methods of measurement on which the index numbers were based, but public acceptance was not, however, to be sought at the risk of oversimplifying the index. Several delegates noted that advisory committees of trade unions and employers' representatives often proved helpful in securing public acceptance of the index.

In the interest of retaining public confidence, it was considered advisable in some instances to undertake family budget inquiries more often than required by theory for purposes of weight revision, so as to have current evidence of the reliability and up-to-dateness of the series; the usefulness of aggregate consumption or sales data, as well as the advantages of frequent small sample surveys of family expenditure, to check both the reliability and the continuing validity of consumption patterns based on large scale family expenditure surveys, were underlined.

The Conference reviewed the usefulness of family expenditure surveys conducted to provide weighting factors for consumer price indices and confirmed that such surveys should be
comprehensive, covering groups of families differing by family
size, income levels socio-economic characteristics, etc. Expenditure patterns might be derived from special expenditure
surveys covering distinct family groups, socio-economic groups
and geographical groups, but in most cases it would be found
preferable to undertake broad family expenditure surveys which
could be analyzed to determine the various categories of the
population for which separate consumer price index numbers
should be computed.

The draft resolution presented in the Office report contained no reference to other sources of weighting factors than
family expenditure surveys, but the Conference drew attention
in its final resolution to the fact that general consumer price
index numbers for the entire population might also be weighted
on the basis of comprehensive information on retail sales or
on private consumption expenditure as a component of national
accounts. These sources would, however, often lack the neces-
say detail for weighting purposes and it might be necessary to
supplement the information by data obtained from family expenditure surveys.

There was widespread agreement on the need for revision of
the index at intervals of five to ten years, on the basis of
large-scale family expenditure surveys. Some participants reported satisfactory experience with frequent or continuous small
sample surveys of family expenditures which could be used to
revise the series of weights at short intervals. This method
was also recorded as permitting the use of consumption data
averaged over three or four years so that the effects of tem-
porary abnormalities of any given year might be smoothed out.

It was recognized that the appropriate length to the interim
period between major weight revisions depended on the social
and economic situation in each country.

The Conference recommended that the list of items to be
priced and the list of outlets from which such prices were to
be obtained be comprehensive, so as to provide the basic price
data needed for the computation of price indices for each of
the population groups retained.

Although there was a consensus in favour of introducing
more scientific sampling methods in the establishment and maintenance of consumer price index numbers in order to enhance
their reliability, it was recognized that probability sampling
methods were difficult to apply. Procedural errors were considered more important than those due to sampling variations,
particularly as they might affect the accuracy of the price information, which was the most important element in the index.
Two main sources of procedural error were singled out: (a) lack
of precise specifications for commodities to be priced, and
(b) the common and often important differences between prices
as observed for index purposes and actual transaction prices
paid by the consumer. Indexmakers should strive to reduce or
eliminate these and other sources of procedural error through
further standardization of the collection and data-processing
techniques. Stress was also laid on the need for frequent revision of the outlet and item samples in order to keep them
abreast of the changing buying and consumption habits of the
index population. It was agreed that probability methods, although difficult to apply in the selection of commodity and outlet samples, should result in more accurate index measurements,
and had the added virtue of permitting the calculation of the
sampling error.

The exchange of views on the problem of quality changes
led the Conference to abandon the detailed suggestions of the
Office on this point, although it was generally agreed that
quality change constituted an important problem. It was noted
that the assessment of quality changes should be approached on
the basis of simple, objective criteria, since more sophisticated
approaches might introduce elements of ambiguity and subjectivity
in index measurement. Nevertheless, research on certain modern
techniques for factoring out quality changes from price changes,
such as the hedonic price index number technique, should be continued. It was noted that some procedures, such as methods of
linking in products when quality changes occur, must be applied
with care to avoid a possible downward bias in the index. It
was concluded that detailed advice regarding adjustment techniques for quality change according to current practice could
not be embodied in an international recommendation but should
rather be dealt with in a manual or handbook on index methods
and procedures.

The question of the appearance of new products, on which
the draft resolution presented by the Office also contained detailed suggestions, was examined as one which could hardly be
dissociated from the problem of quality changes. Thus, one of
the most important index problems relating to the appearance
of new products was that which arose when the quality difference between old and new products was not in proportion to
their price difference. The Conference recognized that in view
of the differences in national practices and the many contro-
versial points of principle which had not yet been satisfactorily
settled regarding the treatment of new commodities, its recommendations should be expressed in general terms, embodying two
basic criteria for the introduction into the index of new products: (a) their acceptance by the consumer, and (b) their
role as significant and continuing elements of expenditure.

The Sixth International Conference of Labour Statisticians
(Montreal, 1947) had recommended that, if price differences between different seasons were substantial, it would not be advisable to use uncorrected price figures or constant weights
all through the year. The Tenth Conference recommended that
consideration might be given to the use of seasonally varying
weights or seasonally adjusted price relatives, or to both, but
noted that national experience over the last 15 years had shown
that such methods might give rise to considerable difficulties,
both of application and of interpretation. Attention was drawn
to another aspect of seasonality, that is the possible application of seasonal adjustment factors to the series themselves,
in order to smooth out or eliminate the seasonal behaviour of
consumer price index numbers.

The Conference was reluctant to endorse the so-called use
or consumption value approach in dealing with consumer durables
(other than housing). While admitting that this method constituted a theoretically feasible way of handling the problem,
the delegates generally held the opinion that great difficulty
would be experienced in attempting to distinguish between in-
vestment and consumption value. For the sake of objectivity it
was deemed preferable to treat purchase value as consumption
value, expressed as full purchase value (net of trade-ins) of
durable goods or as total outlay (including both cash purchases
and installments paid) on such goods by the reporting consumers
during the reference period.

The Sixth International Conference of Labour Statisticians
(Montreal, August 1947) had not formulated explicit recommendations regarding the inclusion in a consumer price index of a
component for rented or owned shelter. The Tenth Conference
called attention to the need for specific treatment of the
shelter component, as distinct from other major durable goods,
and agreed that the proposals submitted by the Office constituted

a generally appropriate approach to the subject. The problem
of quality measurement was mentioned as being more difficult
to overcome in respect of housing than of other goods included
in the index. House obsolescence, as a continuous process,
also raised problems regarding the choice of weights and of
price indicators for old and new housing with similar characteristics and facilities. It was pointed out that there were
often considerable differences in quality between the rented
lodgings and those occupied by their owners and that little or
no relation existed between the cost of these two kinds of
dwellings. Since rental housing and home ownership tended to
develop rather distinct features, different approaches might
be required when the home ownership became significant among
the index population. Alternative approaches considered for
inclusion of a shelter component included the following possi-
bilities: (a) a rent index to stand alone for housing expenditures when tenant-occupied housing predominates among index
families; (b) an index for both tenant and owner-occupied
housing (when the latter became significant) weighted so as to
cover both rentals and typical expenditures associated with
home ownership; and (c) separate index numbers for tenant and
owner-occupied housing, based on direct observation of each
group, when home ownership, besides being significant, corresponded to housing which differed considerably from rented
dwellings.

The Conference was of the opinion that the consumer price
index should cover insurance items to the extent that they were
closely related to the purchase, operation and maintenance of
consumers' properties. Insurance cost should include only that
part of the premium which covered services rendered by insurance
companies (premium payments net of claims paid). In theory, the
price indicators for insurance items should be adjusted for the

price changes of the physical properties being insured, but the
conceptual and practical questions involved should be the subject of further research.

Finally, the Conference concluded that further research
was needed at the national and international levels on several
problems, including those raised by the linking of differently
weighted indices, by the rate of interest and by taxation, for
which the Office had presented suggestions in the draft resolution. Thus, the inclusion in a consumer price index of the cost
of borrowing for consumption purposes was not approved by the
delegates, as in their view, this outlay was related to the fi-
nancing of the purchase and should not be considered part of
the price of the product. It was noted that in national accounts,
interest on loans was considered a transfer of income and not
an item of consumption expenditure. The Conference concluded
that no specific recommendations could be formulated on this
subject, pending further study. Similarly, although it was
agreed that in principle indirect taxes should be included in
a consumer price index, while direct taxes should not, the Conference considered that further research was needed before any
international recommendation could be made on the treatment of
taxation in consumer price indices.

The Conference also felt that further research was required
on the problem of seasonal fluctuations in price and consumption,
including the various methods which might be applicable at the
different stages of index construction, that of weighting and
pricing durable goods (including housing), and the problems of
quality changes and introduction of new commodities.

REFERENCES*

1. Adelman, Irma. A new approach to the construction of index numbers, <u>Rev. Econ. Stat.</u>, <u>40</u>, No. 3, 240-249 (1958).

2. Allen, R. G. D. On the marginal utility of money and its application. <u>Economica</u>, <u>13</u>, 186-209 (1933).

3. Allen, R. G. D. The nature of indifference curves. <u>Rev. Econ. Stud.</u>, 110-121 (1934).

4. Allen, R. G. D. Some observations on the theory and practice of price index numbers. <u>Rev. Econ. Stud.</u>, 57-66 (1935-1936).

5. Allen, R. G. D., and Bowley, A. L. <u>Family Expenditure</u>, August 1935.

6. Allen, R. G. D., and Hicks, J. R. A reconsideration of the theory of value. <u>Economica</u>, <u>14</u>, 196-219 (1934).

7. Banerjee, K. S. A note on the optimal allocation of consumption items in the construction of a cost of living index. <u>Econometrica</u>, <u>24</u>, No. 3, 294-295 (1956).

8. Banerjee, K. S. A comment on the construction of price index numbers, <u>Appl. Stat. (J. Roy. Stat. Soc. Ser. C)</u>, <u>5</u>, 207-210 (1956).

9. Banerjee, K. S. A note on the treatment of composite items in the construction of cost of living index, <u>Bull. Cal. Stat. Ass.</u>, <u>7</u>, No. 25, 35-40 (1956).

---

*A more exhaustive list of references can be found in International Labour Office, "Computation of Consumer Price Indices" (Special Problems)," Geneva, 1970.

10. Banerjee, K. S. Simplification of the derivation of Wald's formula for the cost of living index. _Econometrica_, 24, No. 3, 296-298 (1956).

11. Banerjee, K. S. Probability selection of the constituent items of a composite item in the construction of cost of living index numbers. _Bull. Cal. Stat. Ass._, 8, 106-109 (1958).

12. Banerjee, K. S. Precision in the construction of cost of living index numbers. _Sankhya_, 21, Parts 3 and 4, 393-400 (1959).

13. Banerjee, K. S. Choice of conversion factor in the derivation of an index of a discontinued series. _Appl. Stat._ 8, 42-44 (1959).

14. Banerjee, K. S. A generalization of Stuvel's index number formula. _Econometrica_, 27, No. 4, 676-678 (1959).

15. Banerjee, K. S. Calculation of sampling errors for index numbers. _Sankhya_, 22, Parts 1 and 2, 119-130 (1960).

16. Banerjee, K. S. A comment on the sampling aspects in the construction of index numbers. _Rev. Econ. Stat._, 42, 217-218 (1960).

17. Banerjee, K. S. A factorial approach to construction of true cost of living index and its application in studies of changes in national income. _Sankhya_, 23, 297-304 (1961).

18. Banerjee, K. S. A unified statistical approach to index numbers problems. _Econometrica_, 29, 591-601 (1961).

19. Banerjee, K. S. Index numbers for factorial effects and their connection with a special kind of irregular fractional plans of factorial experiments. _J. Amer. Stat. Ass._, 58, 497-508 (1963).

20. Banerjee, K. S. Best linear unbiased index numbers and index numbers obtained through factorial approach. _Econometrica_, 31, 712-718 (1963).

21. Basu, A. Consumer price index numbers--Sampling problems in prices. _Indian Labour J._, 1, No. 6, 582-588 (1960).

22. Basu, A. Consumer price index numbers--Some estimation problems in prices. _Indian Labour J._, 1, 926-935 (1960).

23. Beech, D. G. See footnote in Appendix C of this volume. Private communication.

24. Bowley, A. L. The measurement of changes in the cost of living. _J. Roy. Stat. Soc._, May (1919).

25. Bowley, A. L. Elements of Statistics, 6th ed., King and Staples, 1937.

26. Chakravarti, N., and Bandyopadhyay, K. S. A note on the consumption of cereals per adult in Calcutta. Sankhyā, 13, 215-218 (1953).

27. Davis, H. T. The Theory of Econometrics. Bloomington, Indiana: Principia Press, 1947.

28. Divisia, F. L'indice monetaire et al theories de la monnaie. Rev. Econ. Politique, 39, 842-861, 980-1008, 1121-1151 (1925); 40, 49-87 (1926).

29. Divisia, F. Economique Rationnelle, 367-433, 443, Paris: 1927. See also, H. T. Davis, the Theory of Econometrics, Bloomington, Indiana: Principia Press, 1947.

30. Fisher, I. The Making of Index Numbers, 1st ed. Boston: Houghton Mifflin, 1922.

31. Frisch, R. Necessary and sufficient conditions regarding the form of an index number which shall meet certain tests. J. Amer. Stat. Ass., 25, 397-406 (1930).

32. Frisch, R. Annual survey of general economic theory: The problem of index numbers. Econometrica, 4, 1-38 (1936).

33. Guha Thakurta, B. K. On a problem in consumer's price index number. Appl. Stat., J. Roy. Stat. Soc. (Ser. C), 16, No. 1, 42-45 (1967).

34. Haberler, G. Der Sinn der Indexzahlen. Tubingen, 1927.

35. Hicks, J. R. The valuation of the social income. Economica, May, 105-124 (1940).

36. International Labour Office. Reports such as "A Contribution to the Study of International Comparison of Costs of Living," Ser. N (Statistics), No. 17, Geneva, 1932.

37. International Labour Office. "Computation of Consumer Price Indices (Special Problems),"Geneva, 1970.

38. International Labour Office. "Consumer Prices," Vol. I of "Technical Guide: Descriptions of Series Published in the Bulletin of Labour Statistics," Geneva, 1970.

39. Keynes, J. M. A Treatise on Money, Vol. II. London: 1930.

40. Khamis, S. H. Properties and conditions for the existence of a new type of index numbers. Sankhyā, 32B, 81-98 (1970).

41. Khamis, S. H. A new system of index numbers for national and international purposes. J. Roy. Stat. Soc. Ser. A, 135, No. 1, 96-121 (1972).

42. Klein, L. R., and Rubin, H. A constant utility index of the cost of living. Rev. Econ. Stud., 15, 84-87 (1947-1948).

43. Kloek, R., and De Wit, G. D. Best linear and best linear unbiased index numbers. Econometrica, 29, No. 4, 606-616 (1961).

44. Knibbs, G. H. The nature of an unequivocal price index and quantity index. J. Amer. Stat. Ass., 19, March-June (1924).

45. Konüs, A. A. The problem of the true index of the cost of living. Econometrica, 7, 10-29 (1939).

46. Leontief, W. Composite commodities and the problem of index numbers. Econometrica, 4, 39-59 (1936).

47. McCarthy, P. J. Sampling considerations in the construction of price indexes with particular reference to the United States consumer price index. Gov. Price Stat., Part 1, January, 197-232 (1961).

48. Malmquist, S. Index numbers and indifference surfaces. Trabajos de Estadistica, 4,(1953).

49. Mitchell, W. C. The Making and Using of Index Numbers. Bill No. 656. Washington, D.C.: U.S. Dept. of Labor, March 1938.

50. Mudgett, B. D. Index Numbers. New York: Wiley, 1951.

51. Neyman, J. On two different aspects of representative method: The method of stratified sampling and the method of purposive selection. J. Roy. Stat. Soc., 109, 558-606 (1934).

52. Roy, R. "Les Index Economiques," in Etudes Econometriques, 5-79, Paris, 1935.

53. Ruderman, A. P. A neglected point in the construction of price index numbers. Appl. Stat., J. Roy. Stat. Soc., 3, No. 1, 44-47 (1954).

54. Samuelson, P. A. Foundations of Economic Analysis. Harvard Univ. Press, Cambridge, Mass., 1963.

55. Schultz, H. A misunderstanding in index number theory: The true Konüs condition on cost of living index numbers and its limitations. Econometrica, 7, 1-9 (1939).

56. Siegel, I. H. The generalized (iobal) index number formula. J. Amer. Stat. Ass., 40, 520-523 (1945).

57. Staehle, H. A development of the economic theory of price index numbers. Rev. Econ. Stud., 2, No. 3, 163-168 (1935).

58. State Statistical Bureau, Government of West Bengal. "Family Budget Enquiry in 23 Important Towns of West Bengal, Including Calcutta, 1950-51." Calcutta: State Statistical Bureau, Government of West Bengal, 1953.

59. Stuvel, G. A new index number formula. Econometrica, 25, No. 1, 123-131 (1957).

60. Theil, H. Best linear index numbers of prices and quantities. Econometrica, 28, April, 464-480 (1960).

61. Tornquist, L. The Bank of Finland's consumption price index. Bank of Finland Monthly Bulletin (1936).

62. Ulmer, M. J. The Economic Theory of Cost of Living Index Numbers. New York: Columbia Univ. Press, 1948.

63. von Hofsten, E. Price Indexes and Quality Changes, Bokforlaget Forum AB. Stockholm: 1952.

64. Wald, A. A new formula for the index of cost of living. Econometrica, 7, 319-331 (1939).

65. Wald, A. The approximate determination of indifference surface by means of Engel curves. Econometrica, 8, 144-175 (1940).